A NARROW ESCAPE FROM
AN ORDINARY LIFE

About the author

Grace works as a trainer, speaker, facilitator, blogger, work-shop leader and advisor. She is a woman who embraces radical honesty about her relationships, spirituality and sexuality. Grace is always interested in new, exciting collaborations and partnerships (especially in warm countries or on tropical islands).

She continues to work and live in several far-flung countries across the globe and is always contactable on email. She offers one-to-one Skype sessions for those ready to shift and expand. Her sessions and workshops are practical and delivered in a no-nonsense manner, from the heart, with a good dose of presence and compassion.

She is still an aspiring belly dancer and a closet hoarder of all things shiny.

She is available to lead workshops, deliver training and speak, as well as to work personally with individuals.

Please contact Grace on:
        gracepayge@gmail.com

A NARROW ESCAPE FROM
AN ORDINARY LIFE

A TRUE STORY

GRACE G. PAYGE

First published in 2012 by Grace G. Payge

A Narrow Escape from an Ordinary Life
© Grace G. Payge, 2012

First Edition 2012

ISBN 10 : 0620545313
ISBN 13 : 9780620545310

Editor: Patricia Crain
Layout & design: Patricia Crain at Empressa
Cover graphics: Toby Newsome

Song words by Mika, *Any other world*

Disclaimer

In order to maintain their anonymity in some instances I have changed the names of individuals and places, I may have changed some identifying characteristics and details such as physical properties, occupations and places of residence. Certain events have been written out of sequence in order to assist with the flow of the book.

I Grace G. Payge, am not a doctor and the opinions expressed in my book, reflect my personal experiences. This book is not intended as a substitute for the medical advice of physicians. The information provided in this book is designed to provide information on the subjects discussed. This book is not meant to be used, nor should it be used, to diagnose or treat any medical condition. For diagnosis or treatment of any medical problem, consult your own physician. The author is not responsible for any specific health or emergency needs that may require medical supervision and are not liable for any damages or negative consequences from any treatment, action, application or preparation, to any person reading or following any of the information in this book. Never disregard or delay seeking professional medical advice or treatment because of something you have read in this book.

Reliance on any information provided by the author, is solely at your own risk.

This book is designed to provide information and motivation. It is sold with the understanding that the author is not engaged to render any type of psychological, legal, or any other kind of professional advice. The book is the sole expression and opinion of its author. The author shall not be liable for any physical, psychological, emotional, financial, or commercial damages, including, but not limited to, special, incidental, consequential or other damages. Our views and rights are the same: You are responsible for your own choices, actions, and results.

Some of the health and alternative medicine related content in this book may contain information that you may find offensive or sexually explicit. If this information offends you stop reading the book.

CONTENTS

	Prologue	viii
Chapter 1:	The Great Depression	1
Chapter 2:	The Dark Ages	16
Chapter 3:	Opening Pandora's Box	25
Chapter 4:	Desperately seeking Grace	35
Chapter 5:	The Voice of God	39
Chapter 6:	The Fast and the Furious	44
Chapter 7:	Me-Love-You-Long-Time	57
Chapter 8:	The Man Woman Game	72
Chapter 9:	The Exorcism	84
Chapter 10:	In the Hands of a Bitter Man	90
Chapter 11:	The Agony and the Excrement	98
Chapter 12:	Temple Tantrum	109
Chapter 13:	Occult Island	115
Chapter 14:	Saved by an Avatar	124
Chapter 15:	Pharmageddon	129
Chapter 16:	The Unassisted Orgasm	134
Chapter 17:	Tantra: The Sacred Shag	142
Chapter 18:	Size Matters	164
Chapter 19:	CultMania	172
Chapter 20:	The Soul Snatcher	183
Chapter 21:	The Bloody Period	188
Chapter 22:	Sex with God	196
Chapter 23:	Fever Pitch	202
Chapter 24:	Holy Cow	208
	Acknowledgements	227

PROLOGUE

When people ask me what I do, I find this exacting question impossible to answer. I have lived the life of an explorer, bioscience student, consultant, yogini, gypsy, corporate trainer, seeker, ashram devotee, executive coach, spiritual advisor, general globe trotter and inadvertent author.

Late in 2011 I travelled to South Africa, finding myself back in the fishing village where I grew up. After my bizarre, mystical, magical and sometimes scary life in other countries, I felt alienated from my fellow Capetonians. Many people were, nonetheless, curious about this returning native, particularly when I answered their questions with tales of a life less ordinary. These stories were met with amusement, delight by some, while others reacted with shock and sharp inhale of breath.

A friend suggested that I write my story down. What a great idea! After 30 days of furious typing I was asked, "How many words have you written?" I replied, "Seventy-five thousand."

"Do you know you've written a book?"

No one was more surprised than I.

Feeling vulnerable, suddenly wishing to keep private the contents of the file marked "book" on my computer, I wailed, silently informing the Universe and God that I could not possibly allow anyone to read something so incredibly personal. I had talked about my vagina and bottom for God's sake! Weeks went by as I wrestled with my confusion over what had transpired. One evening I asked for a sign: either I would forget about the notion of revealing my story; or I would pursue publication. With directed intention I selected a book from the bookshelf, opened it, reading the first line that my eyes focused on.

"Your life is not a personal story."

It was settled. I moved forward with faith, red wine, baked goods and confectionary.

I had neither planned to write a book, nor to be an author, but the path presented itself. In complete faith with the process of life, I dive from one experience to the next, guided only by a voice I have learnt to follow. Most of the time I do not understand the why's, how's and what's, but a deep sense of inner stillness, calmness and centredness has been my guide.

Having largely given up on most notions of social normality, I find a freedom in my existence that I never had before. My attachment to possessions is largely diminished. For the record, I am extremely fond of infinity pools, feather duvets, 4-ply toilet roll, new cars and champagne fountains. The difference is that now my choices are no longer driven by the fear of whether I have these things or not. The flexibility to have a little or a lot creates a spaciousness I was previously lacking.

With this newfound suppleness comes a quiet conviction that I am in the right place, at the right time, doing the right thing. Whether life brings me to my knees or lifts me up is irrelevant, because in each moment I know that life is moving through me. And it is perfect.

This is how I live my life. That is the gift of my experience. My experience is my gift to you.

No one knows what path you should follow except yourself. You are your own wise teacher. You are your own Guru.

My deepest desire is that my words may help you to reconnect to that voice that speaks from within you. I hold an intention that when you hear it, you have the bravery and courage to follow it. You are not alone.

Grace G. Payge

To the grandest version of the greatest vision you

have ever had about who you really are.

The Great Depression

I woke slowly, the smell of disinfectant penetrating the numbness, filling my nostrils with its sharpness. I became gradually aware of the distant bustle of people, vague noises in a foggy world. My eyes felt swollen as I slowly opened them. Struggling to focus, I watched the sunlight dancing across the strange, carpeted floor and realised that I was not at home. I looked down at my massive body and cringed at what I had become. Was this my life? I fell back into a narcotic-induced sleep.

Gently nudged awake by Doctor F, whom I found to be a kind and loving soul, I struggled to understand him. My brain had completely short-circuited, and our conversation was a blur. Normality held no meaning, for me. Yet I felt unaccountably brave and supported in the presence of this man, seeing him as my protector, standing between me and the dark forces prowling outside the walls of my temporary haven. He promised that the other three beds in the ward would remain empty, assuring me that I would have the privacy that I needed for my recovery.

After he left, I walked slowly to the bathroom attached to the ward, becoming transfixed by the luxury of Molton

Brown hand soap and lotion. Thanking the Gods for my private medical insurance, I showered in slow motion, and wobbled back to bed in my extra large track suit bottoms. Weighing in at 110 kg, I had a lot of baggage clinging to my petite 5'2" frame. I felt my huge body from the inside, the sheer bulk, the weight of it. I had been living in denial, not acknowledging how large I had become. I had lived outside of myself, would look at my size 24 clothes and wonder who they belonged to.

The room was warm, luxurious, with its cream weave carpet. From my bed I could see the trees through the large windows, bursting with new green shoots. It was spring in London. Perhaps something new was emerging for me, as well?

Where had it all gone wrong? How did this happen? I had been living someone else's nightmare, an indistinct, perpetual cycle awash with inherited fears and constant panic. I had not noticed how this way of living system-atically wore me down, first spiritually, then emotionally and finally, physically. The collapse was progressive, but it seemed that suddenly, at the age of 28, I was clinically obese, lying in a hospital bed, and suffering what the doctors called a nervous breakdown.

My mind crashed back eight years. I was twenty years old, freshly moved to London from white South Africa, and ready to climb the corporate ladder to success. Strong willed and full of fire, I struck out with zealous naivety, never stopping to wonder what success really looked like, or why I so wanted to climb this particular ladder. It just seemed like the right thing to do. Years of programming in a private school system along with a religious upbring-ing, provided vague, but seemingly sufficient direction for my life. Like the proverbial sheep I merely followed the unhappy flock.

My first job, a two and a half hour commute, paid an hourly rate of £9 until I discovered that the placement agency was charging £15 for my services. After a couple of serious conversations, I negotiated an additional £3 for myself. Craftily climbing the ladder, upgrading my skills and hourly rate at each move, I progressed quickly to junior project manager and from there to specialist corporate consultant. At the same time I realised the value of being a daily rate contractor and that is where I positioned myself.

I became consumed with improving my work life, constantly attending courses and doing extra work to get ahead. I shared a flat in Wimbledon with two other girls. I would wake early, dress in multiple layers of black polyester before heading out into the dark and cold day. If I was lucky I would catch a bus to Wimbledon station, failing which I would walk. During rush hour I would push and jostle for position on the crowded platform, seldom finding a seat on the train, stuffed like silent sardines on the stifling carriage for the duration of the 20 minutes trip to Waterloo. Arriving, the train doors would open and we would spill out onto the platform, speeding through the barriers, down into the bowels of Waterloo station, rushing to board "The Drain", as the tube was dubbed.

The pace would pick up as city workers hurtled down the escalators, rudely pushing past the innocent tourist foolish enough to stand on the wrong side with a barked, "STAND ON THE RIGHT". The stations were packed, dark and dirty, and several full trains sometimes sped by as I desperately checked my watch, sweated, and wondered how I would explain being 1 minute late – again. Finally, a tube would stop, I would forcefully board, wedging myself under someone's armpit with a crotch in my back and a face pressed against the glass. Expelled at the desired station, I would sprint to the exit, to be greeted by the familiar grey and cold sky. On the final dash to the office I would pray for a short queue at Starbucks, shout out my usual order and grab a muffin and croissant to go. Roughly an hour and a half from leaving home I would be swiping my corporate ID, jabbing the lift button, dishevelled and tired after my hour and a half journey. In the lift I glugged my Tall, wet, extra hot, skinny mocha to go! Biting into a Sunrise Muffin, crumbs dropping everywhere, coffee splashing, the laptop bag cutting into my shoulder.

After work, most of us would head to the local pub. It would be dark, again – it always seemed dark – I felt like a sun-starved lab rat, in some huge and cruel experiment. Four or five glasses of white wine later, feeling much better, I would leave my incoherent colleagues and commute home. It seemed like I had been drunk for years, ordering pizza from the train. Before falling into bed by midnight I would drunkenly devour the Dominos's large BBQ chicken with extra garlic sauce. And then start the whole cycle a few hours later.

My big break came unexpectedly while having a drink at the office watering-hole. In the midst of one of my emotional rants about corporate inefficiency, I was approached, and engaged in conversation, by a grizzled, older Scottish man with heavily stained teeth and thinning hair. As we spoke, this man intrigued me with his dangerous, maverick energy. He told me that he was heading up the British arm of an international team of black belts. In his dark winter coat, this weather beaten 50-something man with a chunky gold ring was definitely no Kung Fu master. I thought, then, that Mr M would have been more at home at a seedy dog track than in a dojo. Sensing my confusion, he added, in his broad Scottish accent, "Doll, I mean Six Sigma Black Belt."

I, however, was none the wiser. Mr M went on to tell me that he was recruiting a high-powered, UK business team. He gave me the title of a book to read before the first round of interviews, to which I was invited. My interest was, to say the least, piqued. At lunch time I ran to Waterstones in Leadenhall Market, bought the hardback book about Six Sigma businesses, devouring it on my long, otherwise gloomy, train journey home. This was a new, super-intelligent way of looking at business, and it made perfect sense to me. I loved the idea, was all fired up and definitely wanted in.

So, at the age of 24, I was recruited by Mr M in a senior role. I had intellect and intuition, but I lacked emotional intelligence, exhibited excessive aggression and had a desire to control. This mixture made me an unpopular choice for the position that I occupied. My response to conflict was to bite or cry. I was completely unaware of the extreme pressures and harsh realities for which I had so gamely signed up.

 Insight: I was chosen for my intellectual abilities and aggression, which Mr M exploited from the outset.

I was delighted to be recruited into Maverick's team, gleefully ordered my company car, took possession of my company credit card, and packed my beloved black Samsonite for a 3-week training course in New York City. It didn't take long for my new and detrimental lifestyle to take me on a downward spiral. Bingeing on alcohol and the odd class-A drug was commonplace in the elitist culture that I found myself in. I experienced frequent full body sweats, all-encompassing feelings of terror and blackouts. Emotional outbursts were a regular, even daily, occurrence. My weight began to increase steadily, and it was recommended that I switch to a new antidepressant.

Each day, when I woke, I would try to find some joy in my successes; to feel some sense of pleasure in my accomplishments. My work performance was excellent, with Mr. M giving me the honorary title of the "Atom Bomb." I had become Mr. M's own personal, ruthless, corporate bull dog, leaving me with even fewer friends around the office. The pressure to perform, with millions riding on my shoulders, was overwhelming. I became a frequent flier, rescuing high level business catastrophes. Sixty hours a week I took on department heads, board members and high-level executives to deliver solutions to crises that were costing millions every day they were left unsolved. One word from me could see an entire team fired, or the end of a top dog's career. It was a powerful game to be playing, and it took its toll on me.

My emotional state began to exhibit itself in displays of rage. One instance of this was during a meeting conducted by a member of the board, a sweet and methodical man, who shared a poem about "silence" and the "soft approach" to life, handing out copies to those present. During his reading of this I became increasingly angry as I knew that he was personally tackling me and my "loudness". Outraged I leapt up, throwing the crumpled piece of paper into the bin announcing that I thought it "a load of crap".

Flicking through a Time Out London magazine I found what promised to be the solution to my outbursts of rage and increasingly uncontrollable inner turmoil: a weekend introduction to Zen Buddhism. Perfect, I thought. I could get everything healed in 2 days and be functioning in the real world by Monday.

Instead of providing a quick-fix, the course opened a Pandora's Box of unmanageability. I felt as though the scabs had been ripped off deep wounding, leaving me bleeding and bruised. I had witnessed my neglected inner child and experienced my wounded self, both of which left me devastated. Without the tools to cope with my experiences, I closed the lid of this newly discovered box tightly, hoping that its contents would be quietly resolved while I continued with my corporate life.

My inner turmoil boiled up uncontrollably. Attending a regular monthly team update, I looked around the room of suited men, all with something to hide or protect or both. The atmosphere seemed hot with the energy of duplicity and blame, undercurrents of anger surging through the air. I sat, my heart thudding in my chest. I began to sweat profusely, heat rushing up my body to my head leaving me weak and unsteady. With a sudden and growing sense of foreboding, I knew I had to leave the room. Pushing my chair back I staggered to the door, hitting the table and knocking a few chairs over in the deafening silence, collapsing halfway to the bathroom. I lay gasping for breath, barely able to move, when the paramedics appeared suddenly beside me, taking my blood pressure and asking inane questions. The BP reading had me hurriedly carried to the ambulance on a stretcher in the certainty that I was having a heart attack.

I was given oxygen, told that I needed an ECG. Drifting in and out of consciousness I found it annoying to be constantly shaken and asked to breathe. In a room full of beeping and flashing machines my blouse was undone and adhesive pads put all over my chest. It seemed a short while later when it was concluded that I had not had a heart attack. I lay there, one big dazed and sticky mess with an oxygen mask. Medically I was apparently perfect. How could that be? I felt bloody awful! Couldn't these idiots see that everything was not alright with me? As I lay there in turmoil, my boss appeared in my field of vision, and in his thick Scottish accent said, "Wee Girrlie, if you did-nae wanna attend a meeting, you should have just told me. No need to have a bleeding heart attack."

I gave a weak smile at his attempted levity and closed my eyes, hoping that when I opened them again I would not be surrounded by beeping machines. As if in answer to my wish a nurse appeared, nudged my shoulder and informed me that I needed to remain in recovery whilst they established whether I had DVT (deep vein thrombosis). I got angry at having to wait, knowing whatever I "had" would not be diagnosed in Accident and Emergency. I ripped the sucky pads off my chest, yanked the little oxygen tubes from my nostrils and left.

I returned to work, but the physical collapses recurred, despite the continued diagnosis of perfect health, escalating to include profuse nasal bleeding. My body was screaming the message that something was very wrong; that my life was not working. I contemplated suicide, finding that it had an appealing balance of more pros than cons. Through the darkest times, I had a sneaky suspicion that I had some kind of a purpose. Plus my fears around committing hari-kari were exacerbated by notions of reincarnation, and the thought that I would return, having to work through the same evolutionary shit as now. What if I were to be reborn as a junior telephonist in a call-centre? This thought was simply terrifying, more so than contemplation of ways to kill myself. In lieu of suicide, I devised a Brilliant Plan to Make Everything Better. It was simple: work even harder; get the next promotion; have more cash; and a bigger car. Everything would then, surely, be worthwhile.

I needed to keep this sinking ship afloat, and in pursuance of this tottered off to my sympathetic General Practitioner who wrote out more prescriptions for more drugs. Despite their promising marketing campaigns the leading anti-depressants were not working for me. I had been steadily putting on weight and was, by this stage, enormous. I thought I might be dying, and I tried to convince my doctor that something must have gone horribly wrong inside me. Eventually I was referred to a specialist, a new doctor to whom I poured out my tales of sweats, nose bleeds, heart palpitations, and head rushes. This forbidding, Oxbridge doctor who looked at me (I was convinced) with thinly veiled contempt, ordered a slew of high-priced tests.

Insight: I thought the illness lay in my organs – my physiology. I did not recognise that the source lay much deeper, in the very seat of my soul.

Some of the tests, like peeing into a large container and which had to be taken at work, were hard to explain,and the programme of blood tests played havoc with my work schedule. The results yielded little information to this leading expert but, Dr Oxbridge revealed one afternoon, he suspected a kidney tumour of causing all my problems. Feigning horror at this news, I was secretly delighted that I would, at last, be diagnosed with a clear and serious condition. It meant that I could hand all responsibility for my health and happiness over to someone else. It meant that my "friends" and family would experience a deep and shameful sympathy. It meant that I could languish in a hospital bed, enjoying the care of helpful, polite medical staff, who knew much more about my body than I did. Oh, how I relished these thoughts!

The test came back negative.

I was frustrated, but could not give up on this line of thinking. I convinced myself that there must be something seriously, medically, physically wrong with me. In this state of mind, I insisted on a referral to a private gynaecologist. He, I was sure, would have all the answers, and these answers he would find in my vagina.

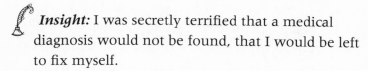 **Insight:** I was secretly terrified that a medical diagnosis would not be found, that I would be left to fix myself.

With relish I recounted my physical and mental woes to my new gynaecologist, watching him hopefully. The seasoned doctor wanted to do an examination and take some scans. Encouraged by this promising start, I readily lay with legs apart while he went down, rubber gloves on, asking me to relax. But in spite of all the pushing, probing and squeezing, the results were disappointingly inconclusive. My only hope was an urgent, expensive, intra-vaginal scan.

Back on track, gown on backwards, down the corridor, I was met in a dark room by a masked nurse. Up on a bed, legs apart, I submitted as the woman slipped a lubricated condom onto her scanning device. Inserting it, she moved it in and out, up and down, and I was disconcerted to feel mildly aroused. Mentally admonishing myself for feeling turned on, I lay staring hard at the monitor, waiting for the probing to stop, for the technician to tell me that she had found something, and that the gynaecologist would explain it all to me. Images of magical pills, operations, time off work, and a super-thin me, danced deliciously in my head. Oh divine joy!

I waddled back to the doctor's office, offering the scanned evidence, waiting patiently for him to give me the awful prognosis. Indeed, Mr Gynaecologist informed me, there was a polycystic ovarian something or other, consisting of some thirty small cysts on each ovary. I leaned forward, waiting for the rest.

"You have to lose weight," he said.

I waited for more, a plan that included the magic pills and the operation. That was how, he continued, I could heal.

"But," I blustered, "I don't eat enough to be this big."

The Zimbabwean gynaecologist looked at me with hard, steely eyes. Leaning across the desk, in a steady, irritated voice, he asked, "Have you ever seen a fat Ethiopian?" What a preposterous question! I had never been to Ethiopia and made no connection between that unfortunate country and my ovaries. He was done, writing out a prescription and unceremoniously shooing me out of his office. Clutching the precious little piece of paper tightly to my chest, I held on to the small hope that the new drug that he prescribed would provide what I was looking for.

I stopped at the vending machine in the hospital foyer selecting 'F2' (Mars Bar) and 'B6' (Diet Coke), studying the list of doctors on the board while I chewed and sipped, hoping to find someone who would save me. But no name jumped out at me.

My still new and shiny black VW motored me home through the cold, inhospitable night. I had worked incredibly hard to get this car, at the expense of so much else, but her plush luxury had almost immediately lost its capacity to comfort me.

Completely deflated, I lay about in bed for days at a time, once sleeping solidly from Friday night through to Monday morning. In spite of my apathy, I managed to get myself out of bed for a "South Africans in London" networking evening to which I had been invited. The details of how I succeeded to rouse myself are hazy, but I remember finding it imperative that I have a professional wash and blow dry. First impressions and all that.

Arriving at the South-West London hotel where the event was taking place, I joined the throng of smartly-suited, mainly male, South Africans. Emphasising my senior position at one of the "world's largest financial institutions", making some small talk, I failed miserably to connect with anyone on a meaningful level. The guest speaker was charismatic, but I registered little that he was saying, remembering nothing of his speech. That is, until he barked, "If you are not your mind, and you are not your body, who are you?"

Everyone looked blank. We split into groups to discuss this question. There were eight in the group that I found myself in, none of us with an answer for this simple, but strangely unsettling question.

My brain reeled, if "I" was not my body, and "I" was not my mind, then who the hell was "I"?

Surely "I" was just "me"? But then who was the "me"? Maybe I could ask my doctor for a pill that would solve this confusion, I wondered, when a good-looking, but egotistical, city boy (to whom I had taken an instant dislike) said something about atavistic memory. He was not sure exactly what it was, but thought it had something to do with our subconscious minds being linked to our ancestors. That we had information stored in our subconscious that we had not consciously put there. As if we had been programmed.

The rest of us stared at him. How utterly New Age, weird and scary to think that we might not be entirely in control, and that we maybe, somehow, carried the beliefs and traumas belonging to our ancestors. I couldn't make sense of any of this, developing a severe headache. Obviously my blood sugar was low, I thought, my head feeling as though it would split open. Gravitating to the bar after the groups dispersed, I ordered a customary glass of wine, large, and some roasted nuts. I spotted the guest speaker engaged in conversation with a gorgeous blonde a few bar stools away. The blonde radiated confidence and wealth. She looked like the kind of woman who had her life in order and I disliked her intensely. Standing there, drinking my wine and eating my nuts, I had the sudden revelation that I was tightly, if metaphorically, strapped to a treadmill, on which the speed and incline were set too high and too steep for me to cope with. The mental image conjured up was so powerful and immediate that I felt sweaty, about to lose control.

I had an overwhelming impulse to talk to these two people. Panicked, I accosted the speaker and his blonde companion, rudely breaking into their conversation. Gushing my treadmill vision, I was certain that what I had to say was infinitely more significant than the conversation they were already having. After a short pause, while I waited expectantly, the blonde said, "I think you need a female therapist," handing me her card. Unimpressed, and insulted, I put her business card into my designer handbag, along with a mental note to discard it later.

Back at work, though, I gave her suggestion consideration. About four months previously, Maverick had summarily left the building of one of the world's leading financial institutions. This left me facing a hostile work crew and a new boss with the smiling face of a cherub and the personality of Attila the Hun. Without Maverick's protection I was a lamb amongst wolves. I could almost feel their hot, hungry breath on my vulnerable jugular. Since her appointment, the primary task of my new boss seemed to be my demise. I lived out of my faithful black Samsonite, eating restaurant food, in hotels across the country. There was no predictability to my schedule, with projects scattered across multiple business areas and locations. I was being micromanaged into the ground, knowing that I could never meet her expectations, or form any sustainable working relationships within the company.

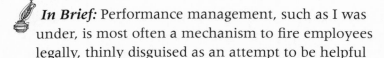 *In Brief:* Performance management, such as I was under, is most often a mechanism to fire employees legally, thinly disguised as an attempt to be helpful

to the targeted individuals. Spiritually unevolved corporates give little thought or allegiance to the "true" care of their employees. And I was firmly entrenched in one such company.

Two weeks after my chance meeting with the blonde therapist, I found myself in her warm, safe rooms, my career falling apart. A week later I was in hospital, being woken by the gentle Doctor F. Booking me off work for six months, he was the first specialist to recognise the impact work stress was having on my endocrine system, not to mention the toll being taken on my nervous system by repeat prescriptions of multiple drugs. He was a wonderful, holistic doctor, who encouraged the use of complementary therapists, supporting my psychotherapy wholeheartedly. He listened in horror to the office-political manoeuvring that had exacerbated my condition. Listening to myself speak I realised I should "go American" and file a lawsuit.

As I lay in my hospital bed, I looked at the gifts that had poured in from my suddenly concerned superiors, including the cosmically huge bunch of flowers from Attila. But it was all too little, too late, the decision was made. The only way for me to express myself and be heard was by means of a lawsuit, which I filed in due course. I was now an angry, wounded soldier, struck down by "friendly fire", and I wanted someone's head on a stick.

2

The Dark Ages

So, with a breakdown behind me and a lawsuit in motion, I spent the next six months in my flat in Wimbledon, regularly seeing my therapist, and ordering a lot of take out. I felt that I had successfully erected a few boundaries, albeit tentative ones, but clung onto the belief that the key to recovery lay outside of myself. This changed when KL, my therapist, observed that I never mentioned myself. I was too busy in everyone else's world, trying to fix them, blame them, and gossip about them. I could be disgusted by their behaviour, had been devastated and emotionally mutilated by them. I cast myself as the victim, and played the role perfectly.

Insights: I did not know that I was deep in the throes of fighting my shadow; my shadow being reflected in all those things around me, distracting me from the true problem, and blinding me to myself. All that which caused a negative reaction, were the very things that I was rejecting deep within myself. As within, so without, and so my inner turmoil was played out perfectly before me.

It would be a long time before I fully learned this lesson, but the seeds were being planted.

Initially I found myself becoming physically and intellectually weaker until tasks such as working the washing machine seemed difficult, the operation of its knobs and lights assuming overwhelmingly confusing proportions. Newspapers fried my brain with their explosive headlines, provocative pictures, and myriad words. Simply looking at them were enough to precipitate a panic attack. I wore the same dirty clothes for days on end.

Over time, I began to restore some balance by allowing myself to sleep in, recovering slowly from a tiredness that seemed eternal. I still felt bruised from the shock and trauma my emotional body had sustained. Short conversations became possible as I slowly emerged from seclusion. I engaged a personal trainer, issuing this hulk-like figure with the strict instruction to "go big." This led to a punishing physical regime, but it helped me feel a little better. Simply moving my body felt good and, thankfully, I began to lose weight.

It would take another two and a half years before the law suit was concluded, and I had to continually attend legal hearings. I was forced through an internal grievance process as part of this procedure, reeling for days after these intensely stressful clashes. The judicial system did not support reconciliation and growth, being aimed at apportioning guilt and innocence, ascertaining who is "right" and who is "wrong". Time, however, unlike the legal proceedings, was not moving slowly. My six months of fully paid leave was running out, soon my income would stop and my company car would be driven away. In a desperate attempt to maintain the lifestyle that I knew, I applied for a consulting role within the National Health Service. But the first round of telephone interviews left me shaken, crying and panicked. I could not possibly don my suit and return to the daily battle that my body had reacted to as life and death trauma.

 In Brief: The bloody noses, sweating episodes and other physical symptoms were totally unrelated to kidney tumours, an "ovarian strike" or any other physical cause. They were panic attacks: simply the result of my inability to cope with what I unconsciously perceived as a daily life-or-death trauma.

It became increasingly clear to me that medical science had few, if any, answers on how to be healthy and decided to stop taking all my prescription drugs. I would take full responsibility for my physical, mental, and emotional health.

This action, along with the legal action that was taking, had spawned a desire to break free, to live a dream. Without the heavy medication and oppressive work environment, I found some true feelings beginning to surface. I discovered that I wanted to follow my heart, and my heart wanted to do something out of the box. I wanted to be brave, was overcome with a desire to do something that totally fascinated me. Since I had loved biology at school and I watched a lot of CSI, it seemed a logical decision to enrol for an honours degree in forensic biology at an English University.

This may not seem an obvious conclusion to arrive at, but, at the time, it felt like the only option. I would be qualified at the end of the course, I reasoned, for a relatively low stress occupation that would occupy my thousand mile an hour mind.

 Insight: This was an elaborate exercise in avoidance. I would do anything that would keep me from fully embarking on the inner journey that I had tentatively begun. Anything to keep me in my head and out of my heart. I was still denying the fact that I had soul that needed to be nourished and recognised.

My applications to numerous universities were summarily declined, citing my lack of previous scientific study. With only a private school education under my belt, acquired aeons ago in another country, this was to be expected, but I was not going to allow this minor issue to become an obstacle. I made an appointment to see an admitting lecturer at my University of choice, whose Bioscience department ranked in the top quartile of British universities.

On the day of the interview, I entered the Bioscience department and was immediately struck by the smell. The labs had a distinct odour – an acrid, musty, humid smell – which I would later learn was mainly caused by bacteria growing in Petri dishes and flasks. Students passed me on the stairs, the professionalism indicated by their white coats belied by the word "twat" written boldly on the back of one, with another sporting a drawing of a penis. Passing rooms with ominous, yellow, radioactivity stickers, accompanied by large, red DO NOT ENTER signs on the doors,

I was pleasantly intimidated. With growing trepidation I navigated the long, polished corridors toward my interview.

The door was answered by a kind, gentle-looking man. I stared in surprise. He looked quite young, early 40's, had an earring in one ear, spiky dark hair and wore trendy clothes. Personal photographs were displayed in his office, the furnishings including big metal filing cabinets and lots of pot plants. An hour later, he offered me a place on the Forensic Biology course, agreeing that my city career and work experience were a viable and suitable substitute for the science that I'd failed to study twelve years ago. I was articulate, extremely bright, dedicated and persuasive and he could see that. But he also needed to fill places with students that would finish the full 3 years, as once a student dropped out, the fees also stopped. He felt strongly I would go the distance, such was the strength of my conviction.

Now I had to tell Mummy June, Dad, and my brother Don. I drove up to Oxfordshire, having told my parents that I "had some news." When I arrived I could tell that Mummy June had been crying. Dad looked stoic, and my brother was online, but we all gathered around the kitchen table. Mummy June had prepared smoked salmon triangles, Dad brought out champagne. We all raised our glasses as I announced that I would be leaving my lucrative and prestigious career behind me, to study Forensic Biology. There was silence.

Dad sat down asking, "How on earth will you fund that?"

Mummy June whooped around the kitchen with, "Darling that's marvellous, simply marvellous!"

Don said, "Cool!" probably thinking of the nubile, young female scientists whom I'd befriend.

Two weeks before the start of my new life as a mature student, my company car was driven away; I replaced it with a £500 VW Vento. My brother called it "Vernon the Ventricle" in keeping with my life's new biological theme. Vernon's plus points were that the rust was really only visible at the back of car, the exhaust was still a good three inches off the tarmac, and the deep boot would fit at least eight bodies, if the need ever arose. It had genuinely comfortable seats, electric windows and a sunroof that added a hint of luxury to my new-found freedom.

In September, equipped only with some jeans, cheap jumpers and a textbook on the human genome, I waved goodbye to Wimbledon and Vernon and I set off to discover the world of Biology, the science of life.

The first day at university found me sitting in a lecture hall with dull walls and bright blue seats, surrounded by pasty-faced 18-year-olds. The approximately 100 students had scattered themselves evenly through the large hall, leaving at least 5 seats in between them and the next person. With my pencil box and notebook arranged on the desk in front of me and butterflies in my tummy, it gradually dawned on me that I was now an undergraduate, in a University, studying something I knew nothing about.

The question, "What the hell am I doing here," was followed quickly with, "Sweet lord, I DO NOT BELONG HERE!"

These were recurring thoughts that I was to entertain regularly over the next couple of years. I panicked as our biochemistry lecturer entered the room. He spoke quickly in a language that I only vaguely recognized. What if I had the wrong room, had I drifted unwittingly into an advanced foreign language lecture? The lecture was, indeed, in

English and seemed to be on the subject of protein folding. Visions of turkey subs and chicken burgers floated through my mind, but the lecturer was rambling on about molecules, amino acids, disulphide bonds and the like. Sweat formed on my top lip and brow as I realized that this was not going to be as easy as I had thought. My first lecture rolled into my hundredth and over the next three years I formed acquaintances, studied hard, spent a lot of time in laboratories doing experiments and scrubbing my hands with disinfectant. I enjoyed what I experienced as a relaxed routine, leaving the stress of city behind me.

Maverick, meanwhile, had moved onward and upward, wanting his corporate bulldog back. This meant that I funded my degree by working as a part-time city consultant during vacations, and when really lucky, managed to secure retainers. This work was even more stressful as my new role was that of a corporate troubleshooter, but I had the secure and safe bubble of the University to run back to. I settled into University life, finding comfort in the simple routine, soaking my brain in information, and relished not having anyone to whom I had to report. I continued with therapy, and recognised my need to learn some life skills. I thought that NLP (Neuro Linguistic Programming) would be a good starting point, and add another string to my growing bow. I chose NLP because it was popular, it was "now", it was "happening" and it paid well.

As luck would have it the very man who laid claim to co-founding the new science of NLP was coming to London, and I embarked on his expensive certification course. Each session began with RB exploding onto the stage, swaggering back and forth in black leather accompanied by loud music and hysterical clapping. He was big, with bad skin, snake eyes and an enormous belt buckle.

I learnt about language patterning, and how it informs our brains and subsequent reality.

 Insight: Thoughts become things.

This was such a big concept that I struggled to assimilate it at that time. I learnt about reframing and the role that it can play when someone has suffered a traumatic event. It is not so much the event itself that is traumatic, but rather our faulty recall and constant, mental replaying of the event.

 In Brief: Our course leader knew his stuff, and I soaked up as much as I could. I was constantly striving to learn, to be bigger and better than I was in that particular moment, not content with the "me" in the mirror. RB was manipulative, telling stories for show not for education. I discovered that we use our tools for the light or for the dark. I learnt to listen intently to the message, not to emulate the teacher's example. We are all human, and therefore subject to live in the dark as much as the light.

It seemed that as quickly as it had begun, my time at university came to an end. Graduation day dawned and there I was, sitting in the beautiful Canterbury Cathedral, dressed in my black robes and mortar board. My mum and dad sat proudly rows ahead of me. I graduated with an upper second-class honours degree in Forensic Biology. During my three years at university, I had started several societies, worked as an ambassador for the University, earning an additional award for "Most valued contribution to the Bioscience Department". Our names were called; tears filled my eyes as I began the long walk to collect my degree. I shook hands, smiled for the photo opportunity, and clutching my degree, walked back to my seat. In spite of the applause my only thought was, "What an expensive piece of paper."

It seemed a strangely hollow and empty victory. What had I really achieved, seven letters behind my name, and the confidence to pick up a New Scientist magazine with the assurance that I'd understand at least 80% of the articles? Surely I should feel more accomplished, pleased, warm, fuzzy, and delighted? I was back to square one, except that now I was a "BSc (Hons)".

Yet what an incredible expedition I had been on! Little did I know that my truly epic journey was yet to begin.

3

Opening Pandora's Box

With the conclusion of my academic studies, Christmas loomed with its gaudy flashing lights and exasperating jingles. My mum was shocked and my brother called me a traitor when I told them that I wanted, no, needed, a holiday without them. Just for "me", I wanted sun during my Christmas holiday, and would be spending Christmas alone. It was unprecedented and my family could not understand it. Eventually, tired of explaining, I told them that I could not stand to be holed up in a house full of people pretending to get along, where the turkey was carved along with the tension. Mum and Dad hadn't been getting along for a long time, but neither was willing to address the elephant in the room, their dying relationship. The result was a house filled with silent rigidity, and relational separation. I would invariably drink too much, become aggressive, and begin sparring with my father. Christmas Day was usually a disaster of impersonal gifts, gastronomic excesses and television. After years of emotionally and physically cold Oxfordshire Christmases, I longed for brilliant sunshine, joy, laughter, wild dancing, deep connection, and abundant love. I was beginning to break away from my old, dense and duty-bound way of life. I was beginning to realise that I could no longer live inauthentically for the sake of others.

For some inexplicable reason, I felt that a yoga retreat would fit my new life's theme. I reasoned that, as a single female, I would be placing myself within a safe group dynamic of instant friendship. I had tried yoga once before in a frightfully expensive London gym, and had been utterly humiliated by the torturous, ego-driven stretching competition. But this holiday yoga experience would be different, I was certain. I was different. I felt more confident in my body, and was sure that the open spaces and warm oceans would nurture me. I searched for, and compared, facilities, settling on a yoga retreat in Dahab, Egypt, that looked just right and made my flight bookings. I would be away smack-bang over Christmas and New Year.

Soon I was packing my bags, leaving my London riverside apartment, and loading up my car. Mummy June, as always, was on hand to help me pack and see me off, but she became more and more sober as the car filled up.

Suddenly she stopped, looked at me, and said, "Darling, promise me one thing!"

"What?" I said.

She looked me square in the eye, "Darling, promise me you WILL NOT marry an Egyptian."

I had no idea what would happen next. Ever honest, and with a straight face, I told her that I could make no such promises. Mummy June paled before her vision of me procreating with a wife beating, Middle Eastern camel herder by the end of my holiday. As I drove away in the freezing cold, I realised that these were my mother's fears, not mine, and that I was going to stop trying to allay the fears of others. I had the conscious realisation that I was not responsible for the thoughts, and subsequent emotions of anyone but myself. I allowed any and all negative thoughts to simply melt away, and I felt good. I had packed my new bikini and hair tongs, my favourite song was playing loudly on the radio. What more could a girl ask for? In that moment, I was content.

Touching down in Sham El Sheik on a hot, sticky evening, I sashayed through the airport, a veritable Marilyn Monroe with bouncing blonde curls and voluptuous bosoms. I glanced around to see who the men were staring at, dismissing it as some cultural thing. Making my way to the carousel I found the locals falling over themselves to assist me with my bags. "What a helpful group," I thought.

Prior to my trip I had been warned that Egyptian men liked blonde women. A lot. I was soon to find out exactly how much!

Dahab, South Sinai, is an isolated resort town along the coast, where mountainous desert meets ocean. The Bedouin Village of Asalah lies a couple of miles north, camel treks leading from there into the desert. December is the winter season with hot days and evenings. Restaurants, shops selling souvenirs and knick-knacks, line the coast along with dive schools and jewellers selling Egyptian silver. Stores in the back streets sell junk food, juices, ice creams and sun block.

I made friends easily, beginning on the bus trip to Dahab when I discovered that several of my bus buddies were heading for the same retreat. There was some pre-retreat bonding, and I felt good, vivacious, and most importantly, sexy.

We arrived at our resort and I checked into my room, which was only three stars and did not have a bathtub. I detected a faint whiff of sewage, but was relieved to see that the bed had been made up with clean, white bed sheets. For some reason, I am slightly offended by anything other than white cotton sheets. I unpacked, applied some lip gloss, and bounded downstairs to meet the group of about 15 British women, with one young gay American. The women looked as though they had practiced yoga for a while which made me nervous. Everyone was excited to be there, grateful for the sunshine. I felt comfortable, though, and unaccountably special. Everyone seemed nice enough and we connected over humus, vegetables and bread.

Our days, during the retreat, began with an early morning yoga class, overlooking the brown, uninviting Red Sea. We spent our afternoons on the beach, and in the local shops. The day ended with a sunset yoga class. I exuded decade's worth of pent up sexual energy, not realising that there would be consequences to this. I was naïve, starved of male attention, and had only recently lost a great deal of weight. The more the men stared and paid me attention, the more 'smokin' I became. I had never experienced anything like it before, and I found myself responding enthusiastically to being treated like a celebrity. One night, as I positively orgasmed into a huge open plan restaurant, I was greeted with a rapturous standing ovation, my very first, and so far, my last. I loved it! I bowed my head in thanks, waved, and thought, "My inner sex siren has arrived!"

During this particular evening I caught the eye of a wealthy hotel owner, who invited me to a private party. I trustingly accompanied him to his residence above the reception of the hotel that he owned. A man servant ushered me through the large home, down the long corridor with its locked doors, to a smallish room, strewn with cushions around a low table. As I sat down, several Egyptians entered the room, making themselves comfortable. I was introduced and the man-servant set out an abundance of local delicacies – tahini, humus, tabouleh, baba ganouche, zabadhi, pitta, falafel, lamb and fatayer – leaving the table groaning with food. The men ate noisily, picking up food with their hands, slurping and laughing; picking their teeth and noses, and openly scratching their balls. They were crass, the conversation tiresome. I felt like a forgotten trophy, stuck in the corner, and I bluntly asked why I was there.

"One hundred camels," replied the hotel owner.

What was he talking about? Cigarettes, a local sports team, the name of a bar? I was stumped.

"One hundred camels?" I asked.

"Yes," he said.

"For what?"

"You!"

One hundred camels for me? Surely I was worth more? At least 250 camels! Whether he was serious or not, it seemed time to leave the crowded little room. Which proved difficult as the men not only encouraged me to stay, but blocked my access to the door. My intuition screamed get out get out!

"I have a degree in forensics," I thought, "I can figure this out!" Politely, I asked to go to the toilet, pulling a face which I hoped showed stomach cramps, miming an imminent explosion of body matter. It worked. Safely out of the room, I moved swiftly, a sleek and cunning panther, slipping silently out of the house. I ran down the road, hiding,

James Bond style, in doorways, checking the road behind me for possible pursuers. As my adrenals kicked into life, I sped back to my hotel.

Back in the safety of my room, I realised that I could not tell my family about this offer for my hand in case my brother or father considered it generous, selling me to the Hotel Owner for a herd of smelly, two-humped mammals.

About half-way through the retreat, on Christmas Eve, our package included a trip to Mount Sinai. This excursion included a Christmas Eve sleep-over, and a Christmas Day climb to the top of the Mount. We arrived in good spirits, and checked into our rooms. Annoyingly, mine was not only far from my retreat-mates, but furthest from the entrance to the complex. The hotel staff had decorated the dining room with tinsel, reindeer, and of course, a bedraggled tree. Before dinner, I reported that my shower was broken, hoping that it would be fixed during dinner. The Christmas Eve meal was delicious, and afterwards men competed to dance with Marilyn Monroe. She graciously obliged, delighted at the attention, lapping up the long-overdue admiration. I am sure that our overtly lesbian yoga retreat leaders were becoming a little tired of my attention grabbing antics, possibly a little jealous of the frenzy I (half) unwittingly created. After dinner and dancing, we returned to our rooms for a good night's sleep in preparation for our 3 am wake-up call.

In my room, naked and heading for the shower, I was startled by banging on the door. Probably a fellow yogini, or maybe the handyman, I thought, racing to the door wrapped in my towel. The Egyptian man outside said that he needed to see me. I told him that I was only dressed in a towel, to which he replied, "No problem!"

Something in my head said put some clothes on, which I did, asking the man to wait.

"You! No need for clothe," he said. In broken English, his strained voice holding an edge of urgency. I thought that he was in a hurry to fix my shower, so I let him in, leading him straight to the bathroom and bending over to show him the broken taps. When I stood up, I found him almost on top of me, trembling, sweating, with a wild look in his eye. I did not need a degree to realise that I was in trouble. He was huge, well built, with dark hair, all eyebrows and moustache. Grabbing me, he forced his six foot plus body against my five foot two frame.

"I must have you!" He groaned loudly and despairingly. I had to meet this fervour with equal strength and authority, so I said loudly and forcefully, "Please leave now!" This had no effect on the desperate ardour of my dark Egyptian. I yelled, "GET THE FUCK OUT OF MY BATHROOM!"

That worked, and I must have looked really fierce, because it sent this horny, Muslim man running for the door, which I quickly slammed and locked in his wake. I was panicked, out of breath, and paced the room, afraid he would come back with friends. I wondered whether I had purposely been placed in the most remote room in the hotel; one of the few without a telephone.

I needed to calm down, and reframe what had happened. I now knew that I could erase the emotion and fright from this incident using my NLP training. If I succeeded I would save a fortune on therapy bills.

I applied classic reframing techniques by replaying the recent intrusion in my mind while consciously changing the visuals. The new story in my head went a something like this: He entered the room, and followed me to the bathroom. I bent over to show him the taps, but this time, when I turned round, he had turned into a mouse. Not just any mouse, but an Egyptian military mouse, standing all of six inches tall. In my mind, he had epaulettes, a big moustache, two huge ears, a tiny sword, and thick army boots. I created as much detail as I could for this ridiculous new image. In my mind, the mouse now lurched forward, grabbed my ankle, and craning its neck, squeaked, "I must have you." In response, I slammed Military mouse against the bathroom wall with a flick of my hand, and while he was dazed, I reached for a broom, which I beat on the floor. He scuttled for all he was worth, and with a great, mousey leap managed to escape through the window into the cold night air. I replayed this video sequence over and over in my mind, until I was laughing.

Now I could reprogramme any event that I needed to. Events themselves hold no ongoing power, only the memory of the event, over which I had complete control. Later that night there was more banging on my door, but I lay peacefully in bed, door securely locked, with my ear plugs in. I gave no energy to the external circumstances. I laughed, and laughed. What a powerful lesson, what a gift! I thanked God, my angels, and my protectors for this profound insight into my inner world.

The next morning, Christmas Day, my alarm went off at 3 am, and I was up and ready for our early start. Not a trace of the previous night's drama remained to debilitate my nervous system.

The next fourteen hours were to be taken up with the ascent and descent of Mount Sinai. I had never climbed a mountain, but standing at the bottom, looking at the summit, thinking, "How the fuck am I going to make it?"

was pointless. The journey, as all do, began with one step, continuing with the next, and then the next. I was probably the least fit person in our group, and I found that this pushed my buttons. As a child, I was always the smallest in my age-group, finishing last in practically every sporting event in which I participated. Now, as I began the climb, I had several failure flashbacks. But instead of telling myself that I was slow and unworthy, I chanted my Mountain Mantra, "I am strong, I am strong, I am strong, I am strong, I am strong, ..." Repeating the mantra thousands of times, placing one foot in front of the other, for the next few hours, I began to feel strong. I was not straggling at the back, but was walking in the middle of the pack. Hours later I felt into my body after stopping for a break, feeling that it was tired. At that moment we were offered the use of camels, an offer that I quickly accepted. My double-humped friend carried me a quarter of the way. It took seven hours to reach the summit, but the view, the support, and my sense of victory was amazing, making it all well worthwhile. What a beautiful life! Our group did yoga on the summit and meditated before descending, returning to Dahab in time for bed. That night, I crawled into my bed, proud, exhausted in body and mind, from this small, yet epic journey.

Insights: As I reflected on my outing, I realised that I had solidified some 'Aha!' moments. I had made the vital realisation that my life was a series of events in which one merely had to keep on putting one foot in front of the other. I had discovered the importance of living in the moment, and that I needed constant, positive, powerful self-talk. I had discovered that I could and should

ask for help when I needed it, and that I could,
and should also offer help when I felt strong.
Most crucially, I had listened to my body during
the climb, and so had not caused it damage. I
could simply smell the progress. I was blessed, and
pleased to have learnt some of basic, 'University of
Life' lessons.

The rest of my holiday disappeared too quickly, as holidays do, and I soon found myself parting from my fellow yogis. Once again, I attracted plenty of attention at the airport, and left Egypt on a high, feeling like a Princess.

Mere hours later, I arrived at Gatwick airport, in the freezing cold, and not one man turned to look at me. How could this be? I was a tanned, super-sexy blonde bombshell. But no one helped me with my bags. A little dark cloud took up residence above my head. I needed to see my therapist.

I was eager to share her delight in the progress that I had made, bursting into her rooms to recount tales of sultry and alluring Goddess magnetism.

She looked at me kindly, smiled, and in her gentle voice, said, "Ah, I see your Ego went on holiday."

"No, I went on holiday!"

She stared, and I stared, and as the truth of her statement slowly seeped into my being her words numbed out my inner Marilyn.

4

Desperately Seeking Grace

With Egypt, Marilyn and my degree behind me, I had to pay the bills back in the real world.

My new degree added two new viable career options, both "pedestrian", both low paid.

The first would be to work for the finest police force in the world, The London Metropolitan. I would hold the position of some junior's junior junior and I would spend my days collecting blood spatter with an ear bud and washing brains off the back seats of cars. Thinking back to my first autopsy I suspected this would be a bad move. Marching into the mortuary, suitably 'gowned up' I almost threw up at the scene that greeted me. The smell was overpowering, nasty, on the first bench, the body of a middle aged Indian woman split open from head to toe. I nearly lost consciousness and fell into a pool of intestines, which were spread over the corpse's legs and abdomen. Stepping over a newly arrived dead body, I barely made it outside. Unlike the glamorous CSI, this reality was horrific and nightmarish with not a high heel, lip gloss or good looking pathologist in sight. Crime Scene work would not pan out for me.

That left one other option, which was to work as a robotic lab rat for a large pharmaceutical company. But I had no wish to spend the next forty years labelling test tubes in a stuffy lab, working on the next anti depressant. I lacked research skills, and this would find me in the position of lowest ranking person in the company, struggling along, never knowing what it was I was actually doing. I shuddered at the prospect of this lowly employment with its criminally pitiful pay cheque.

Stumped, I turned to what I knew, looking for work in the city. I hoped that I could rekindle my love for pressure, long hours, stress and horrible black suits. Hoped that my three years off had given me a different perspective. Hoped that my BSc Hons status would elevate my already high daily rate. I was wrong.

Insight: I had no idea what to do simply because I knew little of my true nature; I had no idea what my gift to the world was. So in a desperate leap I did what I had done before and with a closed heart I prepared to re-enter the world that I had left.

With the updated version of my CV, I suited up for an onslaught of interviews. I was quickly snapped up. In a bold and radical move, I gave up the private sector to embrace the public sector, accepting a contract working for one of London's most violent and depraved boroughs.

The dark, unkempt building that I worked from was a crumbling affair with mess everywhere. Personal client files littered abandoned rooms; empty boxes, old cables and ancient computers were strewn in corridors and doorways. After 5 months of working in an environment which diametrically opposed my beliefs and values, I cracked. The heavy and dark energy that pervaded the buildings, employees and clients, was overwhelming.

> *Insight:* At this time I did not know that I was empathic. Subtle forces entered my energy field and I could not discharge the toxic sludge of negative emotions. I could literally feel the disrespect and contempt some of the employees had towards others. The building felt hollow, dead in some areas (which I would avoid), and a place where vampiric energy fed unchecked.

On a freezing cold February morning in 2009, I packed up my laptop, closed my office door and left. I called my boss when I got home and told him I would not be returning and furnished him with my final invoice.

Work was getting in the way of my life. Another chapter had closed and my city career was over for good. There was only one way to celebrate my freedom: an expensive shopping trip with my personal shopper in Oxford Street. As I bounced from one store to the other, laden with bags, Mummy June called. Breathless, keyed up, crying, she announced, "Darling, something has just happened". I froze, sensing the enormity of what she was to say next, knowing that I would be changed by her news. She continued. "I just asked your father for a divorce."

"Holy shit Mum, what happened, where are you?"

"Darling, I could not take it anymore, your father was downstairs watching TV and I was upstairs in my room. I knew I had to ask him, then and there. I was terrified so I dressed up, put on lots of make up." Wearing the bracelet that I had given her, a scarf from my brother, and a picture of her father in her bra near her heart, she went downstairs. There she found my father in his favourite Saturday afternoon position, lying on the floor, watching TV.

"I told him I had something to say," she continued, "and he said, 'After the sport,' but I said, No, I need to speak to you now. He switched the TV off and looked at me; I stared at him and said, I want a divorce. He was silent and then said, 'OK,' and I left the room.

"Darling, I don't know what to do."

I told her to pack her things and drive to my apartment in Wimbledon immediately. "Mum, this is the first authentic decision you have made in almost 36 years, well done."

Insight: I knew we had to celebrate, not the breakup of a marriage, but a woman prepared to be brave. I was shattered by the break up, but needed to put personal issues aside. This was a rite of passage for my mother and I needed to support her like a sister or wise woman.

Fifteen minutes before Mum arrived I made it back from a whirlwind cab trip, unloading Mum's favourite foods (smoked salmon, fresh bread, salted butter, lemons, sweet sparkling wine, a pear tart with fresh cream) and a gift-wrapped, huge amethyst heart, surrounded by gleaming stones, on a thick silver chain.

Greeting each other emotionally, I began to see my mother as a person separate from her identity as my father's wife. She came in, we ate and drank and cried until we ran out of steam.

5

The Voice of God

A couple of months later Dad was moving out and I was moving in. I had a tricky relationship with dad, falling unwittingly into the 'pick a parent' trap. For a time it was Mummy June that I chose. In the absence of money to divide, my parents fought over pots, pans, artwork, the dining room table and the dishwasher. Dad made meticulous lists of items, adding their monetary value and stories of their purchase. Both of them wanted everything, but eventually agreements were being reached.

The David Sheppard print was one of the items disputed. Mum had purchased this limited edition print (with my father's money, he pointed out) many moons ago, back in South Africa. Dad's argument was that he had paid for everything and my mother had never worked. He ignored the rebuttal that raising and having children was a full time job for which she was not paid. The print was a beautiful study of an enormous elephant in the African bush and it hung in their kitchen. The battle of the print went on for weeks but eventually Mum tearfully handed over the picture.

From outside I saw how little these two people knew about each other, despite having spent the better part of a lifetime together. Deep unhealed wounds of the past were thrown into the present moment. Communication was fraught with malice, blame, guilt and shame. It ended badly; they have not spoken to each other since then.

Living with Mum, a little broken, she a little broken too, divine synchronicity was at work, as always. I had no work to get up for, no career mapped out before me, so we read the same books, listened to Pod Casts and TED talks on a wide range of self help topics. I loved reading, devouring books by authors like Deepak Chopra, Eckhart Tolle, Cheryl Richardson, Caroline Myss, Greg Braden, Bruce Lipton, Dr Wayne Dwyer, Dr Northrup, Louise Hay, Doreen Virtue, Oriah Mountain Dreamer, Dr D Martini, Anthony Robbins, Dan Millman – the list goes on. I understood the concepts in these books on an intellectual level, yet my life was Miserable and Meaningless. I was frustrated; I did not want to read about this stuff, I wanted to become this stuff. I prayed and shouted and cried to the Gods, sending my wishes to heaven. Four days later I received a sign.

Insight: Little did I know that my earnest requests set in motion the biggest roller coaster ride of my life, one that would take me to the depths of my soul and change me forever.

Lying on my bed, staring at the ceiling, I heard the voice. "Get clean," it said. I blinked and heard it again, "Get clean!" I sniffed my armpits. This was not what it meant. "The answer is energy," the strange voice said, coming from nowhere.

Insight: The voice was not audible, it emerged as a "sixth sense". I was able to hear this voice because, for a couple of seconds, my mind had become still. More importantly I was receptive (and desperate). My life was a blank canvas, on which a new life picture could emerge.

I racked my brain for meaning, the rational interpretation for this odd message. Logic was not a means to solve this problem, doubly confusing because I had heard both a statement and an answer to a question that I had not registered asking.

I was resistant to the message, because I thought my answers would come in a different way. I thought my answer would be a new life, perhaps handed to me on a platter by a wealthy man. Rather than a voice in my head, I wanted a detailed project plan, with milestones and a risk register. This six-sense nonsense irritated me. Perhaps I should ignore this momentary split with sanity and continue with my meaningless existence. But I felt a pulsating urge in the core of my being, wanted to honour this and somehow "get clean."

Insights: The more I thought about this message, I more I began attracting people and situations that would help me put together the next piece in my puzzle.

Several weeks earlier I had an inexplicable urge to do yoga, and to do it with a particular teacher with whom I had been put in touch. Contacting Fiona, I agreed that I would attend a yoga class she was running an hour's drive away. Dressed in my idea of yoga-appropriate clothing, I found the studio warm with candles, the atmosphere peaceful and serene. Fiona's face had the glow of an angel, I looked at her lithe body hoping yoga was not going to be too difficult. Her class was anything but, and I truly felt my body as I had not for a very long time. I felt the energy inside, my feet warm and my body glowing with peace and a sense of connectedness. Wow!

Fiona and I became friends and it was during a visit to Mum's house in Oxford that she mentioned "getting clean" at a fasting spa in Thailand. My brain kicked into high alert, alarm bells ringing, timers going off: I had just heard the words "get clean". I wanted to know more, my instinct and intuition screaming, "Listen closely!" Fiona spoke about having been to a place to relax and detoxify. The fasting Spa, on an Island called Koh Samui, had a programme which involved fasting for 7 to 10 days and lots of colema's. I gingerly enquired what a colema was. Fiona told me that it was a self administered colonic. I was simultaneously terrified and inextricably drawn to the idea of this programme. It made no sense to my intellect, but it felt like the right thing to do. This was my first real taste of going with the flow of life, following the path that was magically and mysteriously revealed to me. The more I feared, the more I felt drawn.

I went into an immediate flurry of online activity, checking out details, prices, and comparing everything to everything else. I calculated that it would cost £2500 for a month in Thailand with return flights, including 10 days at a 5-star resort so that I could check out every Spa on the island (to backup the online investigation before making my final booking). Left brain thinking told me that dipping into my savings to fund this trip would be ludicrous. That money I felt needed to fund something, "serious", something "real" like property or an investment. It looked like a fantastically exciting trip. Now I just needed the money. "If you guys are serious," I said to the Gods, "SHOW ME THE MONEY!"

I was in awe at the events which followed. My attention was drawn to a pile of unsorted documents in my bedroom. I loved to organise papers, order and file dividers were my friends. Happily engaged in the tasks of punching, categorising and sorting, I came across a rebate notice from the Inland Revenue. I could not recall receiving this notice, dated 3 years back, for the amount of £2 700. My call to the Tax Man was cheerfully answered by a wonderfully efficient lady. She confirmed that the money was, indeed, owed to me, would I confirm my bank details, thank you, the money would clear in 3 days. I had been shown the money, the Universe conspiring to give me what I was thinking about. I booked my holiday and ten days later I was on a flight to Koh Samui, Thailand.

6

The Fast and the Furious

I love the sheer beauty and magnificence of Bangkok airport. Wonderfully clean with vast white shiny spaces, the air felt a little like home. I was encouraged by this introduction to what was intended to be a month long adventure, boarding my domestic flight to the tiny island of Samui. The airport reminded me of an expensive African game lodge with thatched roofs, glassed-in lounge areas, a stunning big fish tank and flush toilets. The hotel bus transported me to my 5-star accommodation. I made friends, drank and swam, but also hired a little jeep so that I could tour the island. I drove to every Spa on the island, speaking to the owners, interacting with the fasters, looking around the property and the fasting schedule. But most importantly I felt the energy of the places. Only one felt right. So it was that I settled on Spa Samui, the very one Fiona had mentioned. When my ten alcohol fuelled days in luxury were up, I left a huge bedroom, crisp white sheets, Satellite TV and spa bath to check into a hut in the mountains. I really had no idea what lay before me.

All new fasters attend an informative talk. It was supposed to settle me in and make the daunting tasks of not eating for a very long time coupled with self administered colemas seem easy. A video walked us through the schedule of 5 bentonite (detox) drinks a day, 3 hours apart; interspersed with herbal tablets an hour and a half after the drinks, 5 times a day; and 2 colemas every day at certain times. Steam rooms, *umbuku* (Thai tummy) massage and yoga were encouraged.

The colema demonstration video showed an athletic chap lying on a board, inserting a tube up his bottom. This tube was attached to an overhead bucket holding 16 litres of water. The water would, using gravity, run down the tube and seamlessly into one's bottom and fill up the colon. The colon would then release when full, upon which the water would continue to flow.

The evening before the cleanse I was terrified. Preparing to eat the "last supper" at the restaurant I met some new fasting friends. Four of us were to begin fasting the next day. I thanked the Gods for companions treading the same path as me, for the solidarity it offered in times of weakness. I felt astonishingly supported by these people whom I had only known for a couple of hours. I went to bed that night wondering what was to come.

My first drink at 07:05 made me want to vomit. The taste and texture was awful and if you waited too long before drinking it, the mixture would congeal unpleasantly in the glass. An hour and a half later, I swallowed the prescribed herbal tablets. Building up to my first colema, in a growing internal frenzy, I attended the semi-live demonstration at 15:00. By 16:00 I collected a 16-litre bucket, a hose, nozzle and lubricant.

Group hug with fellow fasters. Yes, we hereby bequeathed iPods, iPhones, laptops and Thai Baht to those of us who survived.

Marching off to my hut I made straight for the bathroom, placing a chair in front of the toilet and the colema board on the chair. I hoisted my bucket onto the hook on the wall, placed the tip of the pipe in the lemony water, sucked on the pipe until the water flowed then I clamped the pipe to stop the flow.

I mentally took a step back. What the hell was I doing here? It took me a long time to make my next move; I was not sure what to remove and what to keep on. In the end I decided to keep my shirt on, removing yoga pants and knickers. I lay on the board, bereft, sobbing, terrified, uncertain, not wanting to let anything in or out of my body. Waves of emotion washed over and through me, I was gripped by an icy fear of the unknown.

Time passed, then I sat up and grabbed the nozzle, lubricated it and my bum. I lay back, guided the tube to my nether regions and pushed. Nothing happened. I pushed again, wondering if I was in the right place. No go. My anus had clenched tighter than a duck's backside. I shoved again. Still nothing.

Confused, I got up to consult the Spa manual. Maybe I was missing something. Relax and breathe, it said. This was too simple to be the answer, so I searched the manual for a complicated technique – to no avail. Relax and breathe. That seemed to be the bottom line. I giggled.

I lay on my back again, breathing until I felt calm. All lubed up I breathed and opened and miraculously slipped the tube inside me. So far, so good. I leaned for the clamp and released it, feeling the warm flow into my body followed by an intense urge to relieve myself. This was normal, I remembered; just breathe through it until the water goes from the rectum into the colon. Relief as the water flooded my colon, my tummy expanded as the water filled it. One litre later, I was ready to release, but found I could not. I panicked, everything was clamped in my entire lower abdomen and I did not want to let go, I had become stiff and rigid in my unwillingness to let go of my crap! This was how I had run my life, I was full of shitty toxic emotions and was unable to just let it go. Lying on this board I would be forced to release. I could not hold this litre of fluid indefinitely. I allowed myself to weep and feel vulnerable, then just relax. Warm water and "colonic matter" came whooshing out of me leaving me pleased and calmed. This was not so bad, I thought. The fear of the event was far worse than the event itself. My first colema took 2 hours. The average time for the procedure is 20 minutes. My first day was over, I was tired, emotional and sore. I fell into bed early and slept through, my process just beginning.

I woke feeling as though I had a bad hangover, crawled to the detox counter to gag over my sixth drink. The next couple of days were an intense release of toxins, debris, heat and trauma. It was an emotionally charged roller coaster ride, with my buttons being pushed, my fuse short and my tongue sharp. I was not able to literally swallow the fear and anger along with food, since I was not eating. I had no defence against my emotions. They ruled my life. I was at the mercy of my external circumstances, to which I would react. I felt powerless, unable to control my unconscious behaviours. I was in trouble; it was going to take more than seven days to sort this out.

What I needed was a spiritual man, perhaps in flowing robes and a rosary type necklace, to arrive and take my pain away. And so the Universe introduced me to William, who was giving Wednesday's talk in the open air *sala*. He sat meditatively, pensively, on a high wooden chair dressed in white nappy-like pants with some strange necklaces rounding off the ensemble, looking the part, I thought, of spiritual-guru-man. We gathered around, staring up at our new found maharishi, while he scanned the room with his beady eyes, half smiling, half not. Not a man to with whom to shoot pool or drink Tequila Slammers, I figured. He had a gaunt face and an almost emaciated body. He spoke in an American accent on Ayurveda (of which he purported to be a Doctor), straying from this topic to speak about the soul. I had no food inside me to ward off his message, so it sank straight into me. His words penetrated me and shook me, vibrating and plucking at strings unplayed. I wept as he spoke, tears streaming from my eyes, from my nose, from my very core; I was in despair. My deep longing for connection was rising, pushing up through layers and layers and surfacing in my psyche. I craved a burger, coke, fries and a bottle of wine. I closed my eyes, the cravings so strong, the emotion so heavy, losing myself in the turmoil. When I eventually opened my eyes, the *sala* was empty, my top was drenched in tears and I felt numb. There was nothing left to do except gulp down my twentieth bentonite drink and cry myself to sleep.

I awoke needy and vulnerable and craving the company of William. This man was connected to something that I was not and I wanted to be plugged in. He was my portal to this divine universe.

Insight: I was still searching for something outside of myself to make the connection with the divine.

I had made an appointment for a private session with him that afternoon. William was late (I was to discover that he was always late), so I was totally keyed up by the time he arrived. I tried to control my tongue, but could not control my tears as we walked slowly over to the *sala* that our session was to be conducted in. The *sala* had a teak deck floor and pillars supporting the teak roof. Without walls, it was secluded and separate from the bungalows, with a view of beaches and vast forests of palm trees. I barely noticed this, at the time.

William was to conduct a healing session as I lay on the therapy bed in this warm open space. I tried to relax, eyes closed, as his hands moved slowly over me without touching my body. I could feel movement, peeping through my eyelashes in my curiosity. He was making strange kung-fu-type moves around the table, accompanied by funny sounds. I tried not to giggle as he leapt and twirled around me. This voodoo stuff would achieve nothing, I was certain of that, and closed my eyes, grateful I was only paying him £40.

But I was wrong, something did happen, and the energy hit me hard. Suddenly I was buzzing, and the more kung fu things got the more I felt inside. In a trance-like state I was startled as a black mass of energy moved through me and out of me. It felt extremely heavy, heavier than the densest matter on earth, and thousands of centuries old. In my mind's eye I saw an oblique object move from the right hand side of my body and out through the left. It felt as though it was being pushed from the one side and lifted out through the other. When the session ended, I felt light, I felt heard and I felt truly seen. Not for my bullshit or personality but the very energetic fibre I was made of. And I wanted to talk.

Insight: This was my first experience with the other realms, the esoteric, and the "real".

William listened as I spoke. I said, "I live a joyless, purposeless and irrelevant existence. My work was motivated only by money, but now I am too weak and disengaged to do it. I have no idea how I will support myself going forward, or what my unique contribution to the world could be. I feel a huge empty bottomless pit of hollowness inside me and I fill it with food and alcohol. I have few friends, because being miserable is a full time job. I have no hobbies that I enjoy and no real idea of who I am or why I am on this speck of meaningless dirt, hurtling around the sun."

I gasped as the tears flowed down my checks, on the edge of hysteria.

I continued breathlessly, "I live in a freezing climate my body hates, the grey skies loom over London eight months of the year and I detest the congested and dense public transport systems. I feel like I am living someone else lie, because this was not the life I had in mind."

I finished by expressing my deep desire to live somewhere warm, on a tropical island, with fresh air and the sun on my face every day. William looked from me to the tropical paradise that was Samui and asked, "Why don't you live here?"

What a ridiculous idea, I thought, utterly inconceivable. How on earth was I to give up my life and move here? My inner world oscillated wildly between what I wanted and what I thought was possible. Fleetingly I wondered what that "life" was that I would be "giving up". Small cracks were appearing in my logic. What exactly was there to give up besides unfulfilment, sadness, disconnectedness and hopelessness? I would, in truth, be giving up nothing!

The only thing that separated me from paradise was a paralysing fear of the unknown. In my mind's quiet moments I glimpsed new adventure, but as soon as this surfaced my fear leapt up to swallow possibility. Better the devil you know, I thought, thanking William as I paid him and left for another colema.

I was still finding colemas difficult, inserting the tube meant I had to be completely relaxed, and that was not easy after living a life of stiffness. My rear end remained in this state. After collecting that day's colema equipment, I walked slowly to my hut, thinking of what William had said. I set up, prepared myself, inserted the tube and I was soon ready to release. But the tube kept falling out of my bottom after releasing because I was lubricating too much of the tip and it then slipped out easily. Pushing my upper body off the board to reinsert the tube, I nearly fainted at the sight of a large amount of blood. This colema detox stuff would be the end of me! Convinced I had perforated my rectum and septicaemia would set in, I lay back, wailed and shrieked as the drama in my head escalated. I swore at this "living my dream nonsense" and cursed the inner voice, which I had followed, praying for death to come quickly. But, wait, I thought, noting the time of the month, feebly propping myself up again to have another look. I was menstruating.

Day six of the fast, and I was feeling pretty good. The absence of food and the release of toxins put me on a high. I was filled with energy, my skin glowed and I felt amazing, there were good days and bad days and this was one of the former. I happily went to bed thinking that I would sleep the night through.

But I did not. I was awoken in the early hours of the morning by Something. Something calling me, not a physical sound, but a sixth sense voice. Something calling me to a new life, offering an esoteric invitation to move to Samui. Maybe William was voodooing me from afar. Gripped by fear, I prowled the grounds of my mountain retreat, shaking my hands and my head, trying to fathom how moving to Thailand would be possible. Fear is like a drop of blood, add one drop to a glass and the water becomes muddy. The same applies to the human condition. Just one drop of fear has paralytic effects on life. I struggled with fear but by sunrise my soul had won. My decision was made. I was moving indefinitely to Thailand. Life had made me an offer and I had accepted.

The morning of my last day, day 7, I announced my intention. My circle of friends stared at me, mouths open like goldfish, firing questions about where, what, when, why and how. I replied I did not know anything, except that if I did not take this opportunity I would regret it for the rest of my life.

My new plan was to find a bungalow right away, fly home, tell Mummy June and fly back with the rest of my stuff. I found a compound with an inexpensive bungalow, run by a crazy Hawaiian man named Steven and his delicate Thai wife Bom (pronounced Bomb). She blanched, a strange reaction, I thought, when I assigned her the affectionate nickname of Boom Boom. Steven was to tell me later that boom boom meant *fuck* in Thai. In spite of my *faux pas*, I was able to store my baggage with them until my return. My only luggage on the flight to Britain was one empty suitcase.

Thirty thousand feet up, somewhere over the Mediterranean, I wondered what I would say to Mummy June. I would be treated to a home cooked meal, flowers on the bed side table and freshly ironed, white linen sheets. I was not looking forward to breaking Mum's heart.

Her bright, happy face greeted me as I entered Heathrow's arrivals hall. I had left with two suitcases and arrived back with only one, which I pretended to drag as I fell into her arms. Shrieks of "Darling!" and "My angel!" filled the air, she kissed me and hugged me and continued shrieking. She reached for my suitcase and pulled it, stopping short in confusion, staring first at the case and then at me.

"We need to talk," I said, suddenly blurting out, "I am moving to Thailand."

Mummy June went as white as the sheets she had lovingly placed on my bed.

Trying her best to seem pleased – at least she did not cry – we did not speak of this on the difficult trip home, making small talk in the car. The table was laid, the special meal ready. Dismayed, I stared at the roast chicken as I announced, "I am a vegan." I felt I could no longer eat meat, dairy or drink alcohol. This had happened during the fast, my body simply seemed to become allergic. Mummy June took my transformation from a wine guzzling, animal eater to tee-totalling vegan in her stride, dishing up roast potatoes. We chatted and laughed, soothing ourselves with normality. She, however, drank slightly more than usual.

My mum battled with my new vegan diet, often forgetting and offering me meat. I would be eating a breakfast of banana and coconut oil toast, she would look at me with her big blue eyes and ask, "Would you like a little slice of bacon on your toast darling?"

"It's meat," I would say.

"But daaaarliiiiing, it's only one slice!"

"Mum, they still had to kill the whole pig."

"But darling, it's delicious and crispy." She would say delicately waving a piece at me.

"Mums, it's cruel, I wouldn't eat a cat or a dog, so I don't want to eat pig."

Eventually mum would concede, concluding the exchange with little piggy sounds of, "Oink oink," and a giggle.

My mind was occupied with how I was to finance my new plan. It did not take me long to liquidate everything I owned, adding a lump of cash that remained from my last contract. I left the under performing ISA (UK individual savings account for the purposes of investment with a favourable tax rates), my rainy day savings, perhaps for use when I returned from this one-year expedition. It would be useful, I thought, perhaps for a car and rent. A welcome cash injection came through a stock market investment under the guidance of my brilliant and wise best friend, Debs.

I had liquid cash in my pocket, my moving date was approaching. I had left a lot of belongings in Thailand and was now packing the essentials: OPI nail colour, all 12 of them; 2 hot thong rollers; support underwear; facial cleanser, toner, facial masks (one for moisture, one for deep cleansing, one for radiance). A girl should never be unprepared. More and more meaningless items had been thrown into my battered black Samsonite case. Bra's, jackets, work shirts, formal wear, hats, scarves, shoes of all shapes and sizes, the articles just kept coming. Mum surveyed the packing devastation, sitting on my bed, and asked me to make her a cup of tea. When I brought it, my cases were empty again, all items arranged neatly on the bed. Shoes in plastic, socks in shoes for extra room. Then she started my packing again. This was a ritual my mum had performed many times before. She had moved me, packed for me and unpacked for me, my "proper mum". Doing all those things I was capable of doing but loved that she did them for me. When she packed there seemed to be so much extra space for all those additional essential items.

The day arrived when my 47 kg of belongings and I headed out to Heathrow. Mummy June would spend the evening with brother Don after I had left. The expense of my additional 17 kg of essential luggage could not dampen my high spirits. I was blonde and on an adventure.

I was elated as the huge aircraft lifted into the air. With my old life firmly behind me, I pushed my seat back, ear phones on, ready to watch the latest releases on the little screen in front of me. My vegetarian dinner arrived. The big "VEG" sign on my in flight menu made me feel proud of my new lifestyle, demonstrating my deep empathy for animals everywhere. I positively beamed my Compassionate Green Eco Goddess status as I smiled at the middle-aged Chinese lady beside me. She lit up, pulled out a little silver foil bag, offering it to me. I imagined it containing chocolate cockroaches or deep fried locust's legs. I froze, insisting, "I am a vegetarian," shaking my head. She proffered the little bag insistently, staring blankly. A fishy smell wafted my way as I recoiled at this savage and offensive snack. I shook my head, pointing to my tray with "VEG" on it. Misinterpreting the finger jabbings at my dinner and head shakings, she smiled understandingly, handing me her air sick bag. I thanked her, at least she had stopped offering me her Chinese arthropod snack. I fell into a deep sleep after dinner.

I awoke disorientated, "One hour to land," the captain said, "in Bangkok." Holy Shit, what on earth was I thinking! Moving to an island in the middle of nowhere, where I knew no one. In ASIA! I must be mad. I needed to soothe myself, and I needed to do it quickly. In the galley I found the snack box, grabbed 2 Kit Kats and an Aero to quell my anxiety. By the time I returned to my seat the sugar rush hit me and I felt a little warmer on the inside, where it mattered. I landed in Bangkok, greeted by the huge bright, vast airport that would become familiar over the next couple of years. I grabbed my bags and checked onto my 45 minute flight on Bangkok Airways for Koh Samui, my new island home.

7

Me-love-You-long-Time

Steven, my new and excitable landlord, drove me from the airport to my new bungalow, rental motorbike and a welcome coconut. Perking up, smelling freedom, I sat on my new verandah amongst the palm trees and the brilliant sunshine, laughing with my new friend and enjoying my drink. While I signed the contract I heard a rustling that sounded like a large animal munching. But this was a small island and the only animals that I had seen were monkeys. The rustling, chomping noises grew louder as an enormous bull, the size of a rhinoceros, ambled into sight.

"That's PB," remarked Steven laconically, adding, "he's our guard bull".

"Peebee?"

"Pink Bull" he said. I stared at PB as he made his slow way across the lawn with his huge horns, lazy eyes and noisy munching. Suddenly the door of a nearby villa flung open to reveal Adonis, shirtless and glistening. I gulped, responding to this large man with a twitch in my "lotus blossom" as he strode confidently onto the lawn. I watched in awe as he grabbed the bull by the horns and started to wrestle with it – I think PB liked it – I was certain he was sort of wrestling back. Adonis jumped on the bull's back, slapping him, laughing, stroking him. Jumping down again, he grabbed the rope around PB's neck and the two charged up the long drive way and out into the road. "Where is he going?" I gasped.

"Oh, he's taking PB for a run on the beach."

Adonis and a gigantic bull, running from the compound, down the main street of Lamai and onto the beach, a regular ritual for the two of them. This was island living.

Time to familiarise myself with Koh Samui, my new home, and I examined my new mode of transport, a 150 cc bike. All of 5'2", this bike looked a big beast, standing slightly higher than my crotch. I was a globe-trotting, nothing-stands-in-my-way, SHE WOMAN! So I leapt onto the bike, landing smack on the grass with the metal beast pinning me down as the kick stand gave way. Steven heard my little girl squeals and rushed to my rescue, lifting the bike off me and brushing me down. I stared at the levers, knobs, sticky out pieces and asked him where the on switch was. He laughed and told me it was a kick start bike. Perhaps I needed help, perhaps from a man who knew something about these machines? It was a new and novel thought: that I needed help from a man. So I asked Steven. Several bike lessons and three minor accidents later, I was changing gears, turning corners and kicking my bike to life on my own. I was mobile and triumphant!

I was not taking chances, though. Thailand has the highest motorcycle death rate in the world, coupled with exorbitantly high private medical costs. I needed medical cover, available from the local retail bank, Siam Commercial, which is not a commercial bank at all, but that's Thailand. Inside the air-conditioned bank the staff were glued to what looked like a Thai soap opera, on TV. "Eehemm," I cleared my throat loudly, eliciting no response, not even a twitch. "Sawadeeekaaaaaa," I tried again in silky tones, eyes swinging around accusingly, as if I were interrupting a wedding. A little Thai woman approached me (all the people were little, it seemed) and I explained I had to open an account, wanted to buy medical cover. Medical cover was the key phrase, her eyes lighting up, doubtlessly due to the commission she would earn on conclusion of the sale. There were different insurance options with the "accident and emergency" policy looking promising, but at THB3600 the price was too high. As I pondered the real value of the policy and whether I actually needed it, the tiny Thai lady could see her sale slipping away. Locking eyes with me, determined to close this deal fast, she shrilled, "You die one million you die one million you die one million!" Despite the note of high-pitched desperation, this was a deal clincher. If I was squished between a coconut truck and the wall of the local Seven Eleven, Mummy June would receive One million Thai Baht, no questions asked! About £20 000. I thought it was the least I could do to compensate her upon my demise in Thailand and bought the policy, to the immediate relief of my assistant, Pu, according to her name tag. I read the name tag again, wondering where the rest of the name was. But the letters P and U sat firmly in the middle of the badge, nothing missing, nothing else. "Thank you…. err… Poo" I said. She beamed back at me, busied herself with forms, printing them out and present-ing me with a stack of papers. About to sign, I spotted a glaring error: my birth date was listed as June 2519 and the current year as 2551. This was a scam, I thought, my policy would be invalidated; someone would run off with my "one million". I firmly pointed out the mistake. "In Thailand, year now 2551," said Pu with a sugary smile.

"It's 2009 back in Britain," I insisted.

"2551 in Thailand."

And that was the end of that.

I kept a low profile on the island, eating all my meals at the Spa Restaurant, waited on by Bum, Porn, Poo, Puk, Supaporn, and Nan (who was a man). It took me a while to get used to the names of these Thai waitrons. The food was incredible, one of the best in the world, with an extensive raw food menu that included delicious fresh juices, coconut water and salad galore. I made friends with people fasting at the spa, as well as some of the locals. My diet was almost vegan, little dairy is found in Thailand, and there are few baked goods. I swam, rode around and generally started to unwind, or so I thought. I lost a lot of weight and was a healthy size 12 (which was an XXL in Thailand, bordering on positively huge).

Missing the luxurious experience of my hair being hotly styled into Monroe-like creations, I was delighted to spy a L'Oreal sign en route to Starbucks. It promised to be a real salon, unlike most Thai hairdressers, working from the living room in a back street shack. Excited, I entered L'Oreal, asking for the Top Man.

"Toe!" screeched the receptionist.

"No, hair! I no want pedicure!" I shouted back, agitated.

"TOE!" she screeched, insistently.

The more I pointed at my hair the louder she shouted about my feet. In the middle of this wild gesticulation and the shouting about toes, a grinning man emerged, wearing the customary tag displaying his name: TAO. The receptionist glared at me condescendingly, but I barely noticed as I fell in love with the man that I hoped would maintain my Marilyn locks. "Tow?" I ventured. Grinning at my white face, also at the prospect of a wealthy new client, he showed no other sign. I tried again, "Toe?" Which he seemed to like.

 In Brief: The Thai language is all about the way the word is said, the intonation, almost like singing. Each word has a high note and a low note and the time you spend on each syllable is important.

I carefully explained, to my new hair guru, exactly how I liked my hair done, demonstrating that it was to be a little poofy there, a little flick here, curls down the back, and a rounded bump over there. Then he blow-dried my hair poker straight. Twice a week, from then on, Toe and I would perform this ritual where he politely listened to my excited descriptions of what I would like, he would do what he liked, and I squealed in delight as I happily paid him £3 (THB150) for my touched-up, straight, blonde hair. He did a great job.

Hair sorted, I desired serenity, visualising myself as a calm, Zen-like person. But I felt wound up. I had the growing understanding that emotions can be physically stuck and stored in the body. Was this my problem? Under the instruction of William, the Ayurvedic doctor with the fancy beads, and my own research, I found out that anger was stored in the liver, and I had no shortage of anger. If this was true my liver must need some attention.

The Liver Flush began with a couple of days during which one subsisted on a diet of light greens and juices. The day of the flush itself was a fasting day, when about 3 litres of a specified dilution of Epsom salt water was drunk, followed by a cup each of lime juice and olive oil mixed together before retiring. The trick was to not vomit while lying on one's left side for at least 20 minutes before falling asleep.

Looked easy enough, I thought, preparing for what was to be the first of 7 liver cleanses: eating only raw food; buying the Epsom salts; looking for good olive oil; substitute limes for lemons (the latter not being available on the island); and selecting Thursday to begin. I set off, dosing with Epsom salt water, throughout the day. That evening I struggled to squeeze the limes, a fork being the only utensil at hand to do this with, so it took forever. Washed and showered, in my pyjamas and perched on the edge of my bed, I mixed the lime juice and olive together vigorously. The oily mixture felt like fire as I swallowed it down and heaving, but managing to keep the full amount in my stomach, I lay on my left side as instructed, quickly falling asleep.

My body woke me up at 03:00, the witching hour. I was burning up, sweating profusely and needed to go to the toilet. I made it just in time as huge green stones came out of my body, filling the toilet bowl. I had expected this (although impressed by its scale) but not the high temperature. Rage and anger coursed through me, leaking from my pores as my temperature soared. I paced up and down the room feeling sick, highly agitated and exhausted. When the sweating stopped I lay down again, sleeping fitfully until day break. Morning brought sudden, repeated, trips to the toilet to expel the green stones. After 10 or so rounds of this, I called Steven. Concerned at my pale, shaking state, he changed my sheets and run me yet another shower.

It took another 8 hours before the fever broke and I had passed the last of the stones. I was exhausted. My liver was letting go, forced to release this disabling emotion that it had stored for what felt like centuries. Each time I did this liver cleanse I would experience release of this debilitating emotion, but none of them as extremely as this first one. I was beginning to take charge, to face my inner world and gain some control.

The process had me wondering where my other emotions were stored and how to get rid of them. Asking this question, I was introduced to Mark England, someone my doctor was close to and whom he trusted implicitly. I settled myself on the ground in the *sala* to listen to a talk by this healer who worked with emotions. I was surprised when a young surfer dude introduced himself as the emotional detox man, but then he spoke with an astonishing passion and wisdom.

> *In Brief:* EFT is a form of psychological acupressure, based on the same energy meridians used in traditional acupuncture to treat physical and emotional ailments, but with no scary needles.

Mark asked a person from the audience to describe something they viewed as a debilitating habit, like eating lots of cake, alcoholic tendencies, uncontrolled tempers or an eating disorder. Following his lead, tapping themselves, he led the guinea-pig to the origin of the habit, back to distant memory until their conscious mind could find a link between event and the current destructive emotion or pattern. Mark could see these links where the individual themselves could not, but he was simply too young, I thought, to cope with the enormity of my problems. I was impressed, though, and approached him after the talk. In hushed tones I explained that I lived on the island and wanted his assurance that whatever I said and disclosed would be kept totally confidential. I was terrified that it would leak out that I had problems. He entertained my neurosis knowingly and I booked an appointment for the following day.

Dressed up, made-up, outwardly composed to hide my nervousness, I followed directions to a hut on the beach, about 3 minutes walk from the Spa. In the distance I saw Mark on the porch in yellow fisherman pants, blonde hair in a pony tail and, as I got closer, it looked like he was drinking sludge from a bottle. He appeared to be limbering up, like a fighter preparing for his next opponent, which I guessed was me. Tripping on the first step of the porch, I clung onto the hand rail, my feet doing a strange cha cha of their own, my cool and sophisticated entry blown. Red-faced at his chilly appraisal, I gabbled, "I'm very clumsy, I always trip over things, it's like I don't really live in my own body."

"Hmm," he responded sagaciously.

Hut was a grandiose description for the one-roomed shack with its open wardrobe, bottles of herbs and potions everywhere, no bed, a mosquito net, two old chairs and an old table.

"Where is your kitchen?" He pointed to a table on the deck outside with a blender on it.

"Can I go to the toilet?" He held a finger up, paused and said, "Give me a moment". He disappeared into the bathroom and I heard flushing before he came out, swiftly moving past me to leave the shack. I could hear strange grunting noises from somewhere around the side of the structure, before he returned with, "Now you can use the toilet, just had to pump the sewage."

Gingerly closing the door of the "bathroom", I visualised my mum squealing, arming herself with bleach, gloves and an old toothbrush, scrubbing away at the loo. Cautiously I hovered above the toilet seat, wondering if Mark could hear the nervous tinkle of pee. Reaching for loo paper I found an empty roll. What a Hill Billy Hick! What on earth was I doing here? I washed my hands in his sink, tempted to wash the sink too, but worried that would be presumptuous. I did not bother to look for the guest towel or lavender essential oil room freshener.

When I was done I was met by a seated Mark, the other fold out chair opposite him. "Where do you sleep?" I asked as I sat down. He pointed to a single mattress propped up against the wall. This was not what I had expected.

"Why are you here?" he asked. I can't remember what I said but I suddenly felt his presence. He seemed to exist, in that moment, for the sole purpose of setting me free, all his energy focused intently on my being, like he could see inside me. It felt strange, I was in the company of someone who was completely present. I felt connected, trusted him, it gave me permission to be vulnerable, to share my secrets and reveal my skeletons.

He told me that he was going to tap on himself and I was to imitate him by tapping on myself. He would prompt me with questions and I would fill in the blanks. I tapped hard, I went as deep as I could go, I cried, screamed, wailed, became enraged and let go. I let go and reframed many of the stories I had unconsciously held onto, Mark constantly present for my pain, sitting in reverence for my bravery, bearing witness to my unfolding. I stumbled out of his shack an hour later, dazed and embarrassed by my fickle judgment of his surroundings. Hungry for healing, hungry for truth, I felt devotion to existence and the very process of life. I was determined to strip myself of everything that disempowered me and of every belief that made me small.

This powerful intention set the Universe spinning into motion to deliver what I desired.

I dedicated myself to 10 intense sessions of EFT, which had a remarkable effect on my new found ability to control my emotions. I attended regular yoga classes, flowing into a healthy lifestyle. Tucked in a corner behind one of the *salas* of the Spa was an infra red sauna, steam rooms, a little fountain, showers and a few of tables – all of this in the open air, under the clear night sky. There fasters and locals socialised over hot herbal tea, fresh juices or the evening meal of fresh vegetables and rice.

I attended regular Chi Gung on the beach at sunset, the blue ocean reaching out for miles in front of me. During the organ cleanse section of a particular class, I became engrossed in the movement of clearing my heart area. To cultivate Chi, or energy, I was shown how to position one palm on top of the other, with a space the size of a tennis ball separating them, then making subtle, gentle movements with my hands. Suddenly I experienced a strong magnetic force, almost gluing my palms together, the energy in my hands unbearably intense. I felt like a human stun gun. This energy became a stiffness, my hands twisting like gnarled branches. The rigor mortis effect spread up my arms and into my body, leaving me tightly contorted. Petrified, I shouted to William and dropped into the sand. A thick, heavy contraction moved upwards from my feet, slowly gripping my calves, then knees, then thighs. It was headed for my visceral organs, and then my heart. Crap! This stuff could kill me! With William trying to calm and relax me, I wondered if Siam Commercial would pay out the one million baht if the cosmic cramping stopped my heart. It moved into my stomach, my heart pounding, it moved into my heart and then up past my throat which constricted, and then it left out of the top of my head. Through it all, I breathed, stayed with the sensation. When it was over I picked myself up and lay on a beach lounger, cold, embarrassed and shocked. William gave me some salt water to drink and told me it was trauma leaving my body. Later, in the bathroom, there was bright red blood in my knickers, an unmistakable sign that my body had expelled something. What it was did not matter, my mind requiring no explanation. I was just pleased to be alive.

The days turned into months as I embraced many powerful healing practices. There was a buzz of excitement when Wayne returned to the island. I was told I had to see this healer who could make a grown man cry. Curious, I attended his introductory talk at the Spa, as I had done with Mark many months previously. He spoke on the subject of releasing. I liked this guy, he seemed in control and humble, so I booked a session, wondered how much of this releasing business I would have to do.

The session was to be conducted at my house so that I could just roll over and fall asleep once he was finished.

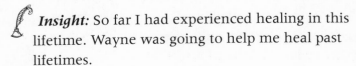

Insight: So far I had experienced healing in this lifetime. Wayne was going to help me heal past lifetimes.

I lay on the bottom of my bed and sat nearby, a stillness settling into the room. He asked why I wanted to see him. I told him something about my family history. I was to repeat what he said, and I felt hypnotised. He began with, "I release the shock and pain of your grandfather being killed." My body stiff, I howled, "I release the shock and pain of my grandfather being killed."

"I release my mother from the shock and pain of her father being killed."

I tearfully repeated each chant, weeping and sobbing as Wayne led from this life to past lives. As my body remembered events from other lives, I felt movement of emotion, responded to the truth in his gentle words. About three hours later we approached the end of the session. Leaving my body, I ascended towards a blue swirling mass. I felt light, transported to a different place. Floating, I saw a man, an older, Indian man, in the corner of my room behind Wayne. I wondered who had let him in. "There is a man in the corner of the room," I mumbled. "Yes," said Wayne, "that's Sai Baba." I didn't know Mr Baba but I felt blessed that he could make the session, swimming in the sea of blue soup, suspended in time. When I opened my eyes, Wayne and I were alone in the room. I slept soundly that night, my being lighter after this profound experience.

 Insight: I had seen the other man with my third eye. He was not physically present in this dimension, but he had been present. The layers between 'this world' and other worlds had started to crumble.

I had now made more friends, a growing group of people that I would come to consider my soul family. I zoomed confidently around the island, in a constant state of awe at what I was doing. I had taken the leap, I was living in paradise, my unfolding life a constant adventure, with glorious people and exciting daily events. I swam on my favourite beach just north of Lamai, where heaven and earth are one. On Silver Beach, my local masseuse, Dow (in my head I called him Dow Jones, a tribute to my old life) would work on me for a small fee while I lay back on his massage bed, surrounded by ocean and sky.

I saw Mark regularly, zooming over to his place, parking my bike in the dirt "parking lot" and walking to his shack. I would often find him preparing a green smoothie. The base ingredient was fresh coconut water and the fleshly white insides. Rifling through his fridge he would locate local bitter-tasting greens, parsley, cilantro, wild basil, limes, pak choi and (at my urging) starfruit – a girl needs her sugar. This would be thrown into his $700 Vitamix blender with sunflower, pumpkin and sesame seeds and whizzed on high until suitably lumpy. Lying outdoors on a sofa that had sustained some serious weather damage, I could often be found holding a gigantic crystal, sipping on sadistically healthy green smoothies. Often supplementing with potent tonic herbs, our supplier of choice was Ron Teeguardens 'Dragonherbs' . Mark had boxes of Deer Antler, Chinese Mountain Ant, Siberian Ginseng and bottles labelled "Supreme Protector", to name but a few. While recovering from the drops I would gaze at the ocean as we engaged in deep philosophical conversations about life, illusion, negation, language patterning, mind power, perception and the nature of reality. If the conversation was not scintillating enough we would zap ourselves with little electrodes emitting our chosen frequency.

On one arm Mark had a tattoo that read UNLEARN, while his entire back was in the process of being covered by a tattoo of a Geisha girl walking into the snow-filled mountains, holding an umbrella with a cherry blossom tree that ran down his other arm.

There was never a dull moment in "the shack" that would one day collapse during a storm. The front balcony would be found floating in the surf, bringing a new and literal meaning to the term "beach hut."

Samui boasted three Starbucks coffee shops, at which I could bank on meeting up with other regulars. The coffee tasted the same as if I was in New York or London. I loved it.

As I progressed with "my inner work", I was surprised at the after-effects of a relativity short but pressurized career. I could not imagine living my entire life in the state I had been in. I tried every available treatment, including reiki, cranio sacral therapy, soul retrieval, family constellations, angel work, holographic kinetics and body work. I sought out the island's acupuncturist, a highly skilled American with a reputation for being "the best". Supporting my unfolding through powerful treatments, I felt strange after one of the sessions. When I described this funny feeling in my body, a weird experience that had stayed with me from the last treatment, she laughed. "Grace, it's called being relaxed," she said.

"What?"

"Relaxed. Your body has finally been given permission to relax."

I had been so wound up, so unyielding, for so long, my physical body knotted tightly with the multiple of layers of tension, that this sensation felt new and amazing. I left in a daze, aware of the madness of a world that groomed young children to achieve. Achieve what? I had been wired for an insane life and now it felt like the devolution of my kind. I left notions of living a modern life behind me as I stumbled to the beach. My cells could breathe as I relaxed into this new way of being, quietly calm, soaking up the sun's powerful rays, allowing them to fill my core.

From that moment my life was filled with a deep sense of gratitude. On my beautiful motorbike, no helmet, no restrictions, hair flowing behind me, wind in my face, I felt connected to the plants and the tarmac and the sky and the sun. Gratitude pulsing from my heart, overcome with a deep sense of belonging.

8

The Man–Woman Game

I began to examine other aspects of my life. Where was my prince, my knight, the God to my Goddess? I pondered this over my usual dinner of rice and vegetables, surrounded by fasters and travellers at the communal table. On my left sat a middle-aged man with a small frame, chivalrous but a touch feminine, I thought. His name was JP, and as we made small talk I felt a large insect crawling up my arm underneath my sleeve. The blighter felt big, prickly and rough, and I grabbed him through the fabric, before he could bite a chunk of flesh from my arm or poison me with a vicious sting. Now what? How to get this ferocious bug from the inner workings of my shirt and set him free without squishing him? I politely asked JP for assistance.

"Is it OK to put my hand down your top," he asked. I acquiesced, and in that moment of vulnerability and trust, unwittingly opened myself to the wisdom and teaching I would later receive from this man.

The beast removed, JP told me that he was a relationship coach and ran a wellness business. I was increasingly drawn to him and accepted his invitation to join him for an art class with a Russian artist called Sasha. What did this man mean, I wondered on the short ride home, when he spoke of the Goddess? I imagined scores of weak, beautiful, fragile women in floaty white outfits, submissive, subservient and dependent. What was it to be one of the powerful women that he had mentioned, picturing a gun toting, leather-clad, super heroine, or a successful, high powered, man-eater. Thin, aggressive, with perfect make up and super shiny hair. Maybe this guy was a hoax because it was impossible for a woman to be powerful and a Goddess and have the knight in shining armour.

As I become more confused, I convinced myself that this man had nothing to teach me. I did not need a man, anyway. I could protect myself, make lots of cash, buy stuff like houses and cars, and I was often quicker, smarter and faster than men. Arriving at home, dismounting my bike (no man needed), I unlocked my door (no man needed) and had a shower (definitely no man needed). I had paid for all this stuff by myself and had navigated around the globe several times, no man needed. I was positively pissed off by the very thought of men by the time I got into bed. Fuck them.

The process had begun.

The next morning JP was chirpy and bright eyed, perky, healthy and coach-like, the opposite of how I was feeling. Art teacher Sasha was annoyingly beautiful, glowing and feminine, with post-coital doe eyes. Speaking gently as she explaining various techniques and tools of painting, she encouraged us to conceptualise what we wanted to create. I stared at the canvas with a pencil in my hand. My mind was blank and the canvas stayed blank. The last time I had created artistically was probably in pre-school, my haphazard paint smears drawing delight from parents and teachers. When did this change? My creativity curbed, emphasis placed on empirical data, measurements, and colouring in only between prescriptive lines. My right brain was a deep void, soulful creativity was something Western society had not encouraged in me. And so the canvas in front of the left-brained me remained blank, and I was irritated. JP started talking to me, gently coaxing my creativity from the feminine, encouraging me to visualise the picture that I called "The flames of passion". I began creating, fiery flames licked the canvas, red hot passion flashing into every corner. A heat ignited within me, fuelling each moment, fuelling my desire. Sweating and stroking my picture, inserting reds, oranges and white hot energy, I was enjoying myself. I was creating and in that moment I was feminine. Shifting, ready to shift. JP and I cracked open celebratory coconuts in honour of our creations, he eager to share his knowledge and I sponge-like in my receptivity.

Drawing on a napkin, JP explained that there are four levels of relationships. The first stage of relationship existed predominantly in the era when my parents were young. Their relationship was one of dependence. The man was the tough guy, working to put food on the table. The woman was the stay-at-home mum who probably married in her early twenties and devoted her life to her man and her family. I studied the napkin, on which he had drawn a shapely woman with bouncy hair and a dashing looking chap with a chiselled jaw. In this type of relationship the predominant traits were a weak and insecure woman and a controlling and dominant man. Controlling men rob women of their personalities and joy, until they feel that their lives are not their own. When things go a little awry, the woman controls the situation by withholding sex, at which point the man would probably go out and sleep with his secretary. He is reliant on her for cooking, cleaning and raising the children, she needs him for cash.

I ordered us another coconut, staring defensively at the diagram. There was no trace of me or my life there. Our second coconuts arrived and I gulped down the sweet clear water. We were moving onto Stage Two relationships and I was intrigued.

Young children of Stage One parents will strive for interdependent relationships. Young girls grow into super woman. He drew a muscled woman with a big "S" on her chest. She was the in-charge, dominant, do-it-all type. She would look at her mum and think "I am NEVER going to grow up like you". JP explained that there was nothing wrong with a woman in her twenties learning to provide for herself, but a woman still proving she was tough and independent looked inherently unattractive in her thirties, and it was almost a disaster for a woman to still be like this in her forties. Boys who grew up with Stage One parents began to discover their hearts, not wanting to be tough and ball-busting like dad. He drew a long-haired male on the napkin holding a guitar and smoking some weed. He filled the picture in with tie dyed pants and a big heart on the T-shirt. Because the woman was titanic she would attract a male with opposite energies, he would rely on her, strum on his guitar and the relationship would be a distant one. She: unable to open; he: feminine and soft; the distance between them translating into a total lack of intimacy. She would run off to the sex shop for a vibrator, he would ensconce himself in pornography to cover his needs. I needed dessert to cover up my uneasiness: I liked being the titanic, ball-busting woman; it gave me immense satisfaction to crush men. So I said, "JP great drawing, but I like looking after myself, buying stuff, being independent, I am never going to change."

He sat back in his chair, pushing back his glasses. Smiling tenderly, he asked, "How is that working for your love life?" I did the goldfish thing with my mouth. Open, close, open, close. He continued softly, "It's fine to be the titanic woman if you never want to have a relationship. You will have money, a big house and a career. Men will probably be intimidated by you until the day you die. But if you want to have an intimate love relationship you will have to move into Stage Three."

My head hurt and I wanted to leave the table and JP, to isolate myself, safe in the knowledge I had a platinum card and knew how to use it. Part of me did not want to change, but another part of me knew I had to continue. "OK JP, what is Stage Three?" Stage Three represented gender synergy. JP drew a muscled man with a big heart on his chest, a beautiful woman with a heart on her chest. He said this woman was an holistic being, she had fallen in love with herself and her life. She had let go of her childhood challenges and was living a purposeful life with self respect. The man had found his talent and his heart, his circle of influence had expanded and he lived to serve her. I must be hearing things.

"Repeat that, JP"

"The masculine lives to serve the feminine."

Better keep on listening, I knew nothing about this stuff. The woman was in constant gratitude, she expressed her desires without expectation or attachment. She was delighted when men served her, even in the smallest ways. She focused on the things that worked and did not harp on the things that did not. He explained that when she changed, he changed. It only takes one.

My head was throbbing, it was time to stop. I thanked JP and we agreed to continue on Silver Beach the following day.

I was confused as I drove home on my bike. This was like being in Life School, learning real things about the Universe, love, relationships, spirit and all the other things we should have been taught but were not. I liked the theoretical idea of the Stage Three woman. I was very much the titan, I had over thirty years of beliefs stored in my head that underpinned my Stage Two-ness, but I had a strong desire to change. Deep desire for change is the catalyst for different behaviour and I wanted to be different. I did not want simply the intellectual knowledge, I wanted to become a loving, giving, divine woman, a woman who would allow a man to serve her.

I arrived on the beach the next morning equipped with my big straw beach mat and a bottle of water, eager for the next lesson. But as I walked towards the distant figure of JP under the shade of the only tree on the beach, I wondered what all this New Age Goddess stuff was about. I felt at once drawn and repelled, wanting to change and wanting to stay the same.

 Insight: My inner masculine was fighting for control as it was the only way I knew how to operate in this world. The only thing separating me and my willingness to embrace a new way of thinking and being was my age old friend, fear.

JP lay on a towel watching my anxious approach with a knowing smile. On a sheet of paper he drew lines dividing the page into quadrants. He marked the top left quadrant "Light Masculine" and top right, "Light Feminine". The bottom left quadrant was the "Dark Masculine" and the bottom right the "Dark Feminine". He explained that, not only do we have masculine and feminine energy in the world, we also have light and dark. We could hang out in any quadrant, as we all have the inner man and inner woman.

The characteristics of the Light Masculine are those of being focused, ambitious, logical, organized, protective, assertive, rational, active, doing and competitive. I absorbed the list, easily identifying with these traits, so I mostly hung out in this quadrant. Dark Masculine energies are aggressive, angry, controlling, domineering, harsh, critical and bullying. My life in the city had forced me into acting out from that quadrant most of the time, and this realization made me unhappy. The Dark Feminine was weak, helpless, fickle, needy, a victim, manipulative and insecure. This was the image that I held of the feminine, a frail lady, mildly pathetic.

What was in the box of the Light Feminine? This box held the key to becoming the Stage Three Goddess, the one who attracts the knight in shining armour, I racked my brains for someone, anything, a single quality that I felt would belong in there. All I could think of was "feminine", but that didn't make any sense so I said nothing. Then I thought of intuitive. JP wrote it down, smiling. He continued writing for me: radiant, vague, spontaneous, caring, tranquil, receptive, collaborative, being. He concluded with the words surrendering, vulnerable and passive. I felt as though my head would explode. These were the antithesis of what I was brought up to be. These words made no sense, if I lived my life in this box I would lose control and turn to mush!

Needing to cool off, feeling unsafe, I swam out to the buoys bobbing in the distance, JP swimming steadily behind me. He sensed the shift coming and knew that it was going to be a big one. By the time that I reached the buoys, far from the shore, I was crying and gulping and treading water. He was treading water next to me, telling me that was OK to feel like this, without my strong inner masculine I probably would not have survived, that I needed this inner man to get me through, but now in my thirties it was OK, I could stop struggling and allow myself to step into the light feminine, that it was safe there. I was howling dramatically, in my dark feminine no doubt. Telling me that he was going to swim back he invited me to join him. I snivelled that I would stay.

"Grace, your power lies in your feminine." I watched him swim back to shore.

Floating on my back, I looked to the sky for guidance, asking for a sign, something that would tell me it was safe to be in my feminine. I closed my eyes, I let myself slowly become one with the ocean, I started to feel her, I was floating in the womb of our mother earth. I dissolved into the ocean with the rhythmic flow of the gentle tide. The sea washed through me, feminine energy cascading from head to toe, a huge oceanic orgasm. I was one with spirit, powerfully feminine, limitlessly available and open. It was amazing, arousing, God-like, natural, and I let this pure energy carry me back to shore. I stepped out of this giant womb and collected my towel, overwhelmed, grateful. I

needed to settle, thanking JP. That night I dropped into a
long, deep and restful sleep.

The next morning I woke strangely softer, gentler, more
fluid and ready for more teachings. JP and I met over a
breakfast of papaya, banana and mango. I followed this up
with a coconut water and wheatgrass shot. He asked me
about my relationship with my father. I said it wasn't good,
I had not even told him I had moved to Thailand.

"Can you forgive him?"

Spellbound, I gazed deep into JP's eyes, my heart opened,
flooding with love for my father. In JP I caught a glimpse
of my dad and tears ran down his face, down mine too. In
that moment I felt my father, I felt his love, I knew he had
never stopped loving me. The only thing separating me and
his love for me, was myself. Later, JP said, "I channelled
your father, he loves you very much."

From this wonderfully spectacular sharing I knew, for
certain, that all healing happens within. True forgiveness,
love and compassion need only one shift, and that is my
own.

What a profound morning, and the day had just began!
The lesson continued, and I had questions about the previous day. I reasoned that if I were a brain surgeon about
to operate on someone, the traits of the Light Feminine,
vague and soft and passive, would kill the patient. "Ah," JP
responded, "But you can switch between any of the quadrants. If you need to do a tax return or want to drive a car, it's
best to be in your light masculine. But if you are in a room
full of men ready to be of service, you are wasting energy
being in your masculine." I was relieved to hear this, not
wanting to spend all my days in what I viewed, then, as a
potentially vegetative state. All energy will attract an equal

and opposite, so if I whined and nagged and hung out in the dark feminine, I would naturally attract the dark masculine qualities of a man being dominant and controlling. If I was weak and helpless that would attract someone who would probably become aggressive and bullying. If I wanted the knight in shining armour to protect, become helpful and assertive I would need to be radiant, flowing and intuitive. However if I needed to assert myself in certain situations I could do that, but only if necessary. In my old work place, I was paid to be a linear thinker, and an aggressive force in the work place. I attracted weak helpless, feminine men and it had not served me.

The feminine craved safety and connection from her partner and a man wanted freedom and respect. These dynamics applied not only to intimate partners, but in all relationships. My new barometer with my male friends would be: Do I feel safe with you and do I feel connected to you? I would give them their freedom and respect and see how things panned out.

Over the next couple of weeks JP taught me how to express my desires without expectation or attachment, to allow men to fulfil my desires leaving the details of when, how and what up to them. I realized men needed gratitude, in bucket loads. The more grateful I was the more men wanted to serve. I understood that men thought in boxes where woman could multi-task. I developed conscious partnership strategies to cope with different situations. As a titanic and dominating woman my ego and inner masculine fought me most of the way. The struggle caused me many sleepless nights, I was very concerned about the practicalities of navigating this world as a soft, yet powerful woman. It was an unfamiliar concept, my inner struggle with it patent.

JP chose to move me from theory to actual experience, giving me a practical assignment. "I want you to remain in your light feminine and ask any man of your choosing to take you out for dinner." He added, "It must not be anyone you know well."

"Well, he'll want sex. What man would be willing to pay for no action?" I felt ill, I had a surprisingly low opinion of myself, which I covered up by slapping my platinum credit card on the table, paying for myself in a triumphant and masculine fashion. Asking someone to take me for dinner, upfront, seemed shameless. JP assured me that it would not end in the bedroom, that I was a Goddess and if I stated this energetically, any man would be delighted with my company and as a masculine gesture would want to pay.

How, exactly, was this going to work, I wanted to know. As soon as I expressed my desire to go for dinner, the man would automatically grumble, JP said. I was, under no circumstances, to disrupt this very important process. I was to listen in a receptive mode, smiling and nodding until the grumbling stopped, this was a man thing. In his brain he would be trying to find a way to fulfil my desire, so he would be "working through the logistics." When he delivered his outcome I was to graciously accept whatever answer he provided.

The more I thought about this the more it seemed like a truly terrible idea, it would be far easier to buy my own dinner and forget the whole business. I loved the theory but the practical seemed too challenging and far-fetched, I was a woman of the 90's for God's sake! JP's voice echoed in the back of my mind, "And how is that working for you?"

The desire to change meant a leap into the unknown. At the Spa that evening I locked my sights on a middle-aged faster called Trevor. We had conversed a few times, so I knew him, but not well. I centred myself, smiling and said, "Hi Trevor, how was your day?"

"Great day today. Feeling good."

"Trevor, could I ask you something?"

"Sure,"

"It would mean a lot to me if you took me out for dinner." There, I had said it. I smiled, he looked vacant at first, then grumbled without a breath as his mind shifted gears.

"Well it's the last day of my fast tomorrow and I need to book my flight back and organize my taxi and do the final colema tomorrow and get my drink sorted for the morning and then I have to pack and I really need to sort everything out and..."

Breathe, I thought, and I smiled and held eye contact and nodded. In the middle of the rambling he took a deep breath and boomed, "HOW ABOUT MONDAY NIGHT?"

"I would be delighted," said I, graciously.

We went out for dinner on Monday, an experience that I desperately needed. I was starting to trust men. I started to deeply appreciate their place beside us. I wanted more in my life, I wanted a relationship with these amazing creatures. Trevor opened the flood gates for a titanic shift.

JP left, and I resumed my wonderful life on the island, although the Universe, sensing change, was preparing my next step. Except it was not merely a step. It was a Rite of Passage.

9

The Exorcism

During a usual "porch session" with Mark, the topic of *Iboga* emerged. I knew that Mark administered this plant medicine to facilitate Shamanic Rites of passage.

Iboga is a medicine, which is the central pillar of the Bwiti spiritual practice in Gabone. Mark used Ibogaine, the active alkaloid found in the bark of the tree. The YouTube clip that I watched showed a bizarre, dark shamanic practice, a ludicrous dice with death. When Mark proposed a "rites of passage ritual", I firmly told him, "You're barking up the wrong tree". I thought that he was deluded. But, one evening on the porch, he said, "Grace, life will either force you to completely surrender, or you can choose to surrender to life. Either way you will surrender. *So why don't you choose the moment, then you can prepare. Sort of.*"

I felt sick. I needed the bathroom. Something was going to come out the top or the bottom and I was not sure which. I had been struck to the core. I felt compelled to do this thing. Three days later I said to Mark, "Game on!" We agreed on a date for the ceremony.

"The process has already begun," said Mark, "the plant medicine has called and you have answered, it is already taking effect." My bowels stirred again and I was right to have a sense of impending doom.

Jared was large, a threatening and domineering figure, possessing neither tact nor patience, known around the island for his straight-talking, no-nonsense approach to life. Jared was also Mark's partner in this venture. We picked a day in which I was able to ask questions about what would happen during this initiation. Mark and Jared explained that I would sleep over at the location where this was taking place, Mark would arrive the next day and administer the dose, I was to be physically looked after for a full 12 hours, then for as long as necessary over the next couple of days. They would help me physically as I would not be able to control my body, I would be violently ill during this process, and they would be on hand to take care of the necessary hygiene-related logistics.

I asked the question that I had been plagued with, "Will I die?", I looked directly at Jared and he said, "I don't know." It was not the answer I was hoping for, feeling a chilly coldness on this warm tropical evening. Maybe now would be a good time to bump up my death and accident cover.

Two days to go and I prepared by fasting, cleansing my system with juices and water. I bought fifty tea light candles and spent an entire day writing fifty intentions on pieces of paper the size of a credit card. I was going into this with a view to opening and embracing the unknown. I was also going into this with empty bowels, so I purchased an enema bag from my local health shop. With one day to go I was a bag of nerves, my mind full of stories of demons being released, men being thrown against walls, people losing teeth and releasing buckets of blood. I still felt compelled to continue, in spite of the dangers. I arrived at the location that night, unpacked, placing pictures of my family on the fridge and sticking the Light Prayer on the bathroom mirror. I laid out fifty candles and under each one I placed an intention. I went to bed, praying for sleep, knowing that I may not make it through the next day.

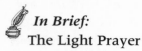

In Brief:
The Light Prayer

I am the Light, I serve the Light, I love the light, I love Myself, I love God, I am one with God.

The next morning I made sure to administer the enema before dressing in white. I lit each candle and read every intention aloud. I became mindful, slow, deliberate and in the moment. As the fiftieth candle was lit, Mark arrived to a room ablaze with light. I had a need to burn away whatever was going to come out of me. My instincts were spot on. Mark measured out the dose and I swallowed this ancient, mystical and vile-tasting medicine. Absolutely petrified, I moved to the sofa. After half an hour or so, Mark suggested that I lie down, things would start to happen. I lay on the bed and waited.

Suddenly I felt as though I had been hit by a freight train. I even heard trains, motor bikes, talking, laughing and then I was in space, and I opened my eyes as I floated through a beautiful night sky. Looking over to where Mark was, I was utterly petrified to see a massive green reptile. I opened my mouth to scream, but my body had surrendered. I could not move, I could not talk, I could not communicate. I could only watch and attempt to control my thoughts, but my mind was paralysed. Beyond terrified, I vomited into the large bucket the huge reptile held out for me. I stared into the bottom of the bucket at the huge writhing, scratching scarab beetles that I had thrown up. As I wondered if it could get any worse, evil arrived. An evil entirely vile, destructive and paralysing, and it came out of my deepest recesses. There were thousands of devilish eyes piercing me and I watched catatonic as these eyes stared back at me reflecting my own darkness. I moved beyond the realms of being petrified, I was staring death in the face. I had lost control over my body and my mind, and I felt that I would next lose my soul.

My physical being felt as though it was stuck in the jet engine of a Boeing 747. I started vibrating out of my body, leaving my being and moving on. As I was leaving myself I felt a thudding – I had lost the ability to feel and I was totally numb – still I felt a tapping somewhere in my energy body. Mark had picked up my hand and started to tap on me, I was forced back down. The ritual continued for hours and I prayed for death, I spoke to the plant and prayed for death, I had had enough. I saw myself lying on a cold steel mortuary table wearing a white and red floral dress. I did not know if I really was dead or not, I screamed with all the psychic powers I could muster, "I SURRENDER, I SURRENDER, I SURRENDER."

Then I was back, suddenly, opening my eyes and looking at Mark. It was over. I was alive. Jared was in the room, too. "Want some more?" was his first response. I vomited again at the thought, weakly shaking my head. It was like the medicine had disappeared, but when I rose I saw everything as vibration and transparent. I had experienced my own mortality, the complete surrender of self. I was rendered physically incapacitated during this dark experience, the most intensely sinister experience that I had ever had. My friend Jo arrived and lay with me, her peaceful and deeply feminine presence soothing. Later she gently bathed me in a warm bath, washing away my fears.

It took me a harrowing six days to recover, and sometimes I thought I never would. I often found myself lying naked on the floor, sobbing mantras of life but praying to die. Forced to face my karmic shadow had thrown me into an existential crisis. Something was dying inside, something expanding in the gaping hole the experience had left behind.

On the sixth day I felt brave, invincible. In a white robe and a pink silk eye mask, I strode barefoot to a little delicatessen for fresh fruit juice and dark chocolate. I had survived an epic rite of passage. I no longer cared what anyone thought. I was connected to my own authentic power. I sashayed out of the store, not caring that I looked like a lunatic.

I had great days and I had dark days, weeks went by and I began to even out, a little different than before I walked into this experience. I wondered what would come in next, hoping that my next adventure would be something gentle and light. But I was wrong again.

Around the Spa, Anna was the "Yoga teacher from the Matrix". She was petite and toned with the biggest blue eyes I had ever seen. I had been drawn to her from the outset, but I suppose everyone was. Her yoga classes were dances with the divine. Anna and I spoke a little, exchanging greetings, and I shared something of my background with her. One night we bumped into each other in the steam room area, the local watering hole. She described a friend of hers as she shared the fragrance he had given her. He was a doctor, a scientific wizard who ran the most comprehensive detoxification program in the world. He was currently in Samui on one of the few visits he made to the island. I should meet him, she said. And I did when I encountered them later. He looked yummy with sparkling blue eyes, charming and witty, and I gladly accepted their invitation to join them. Dr A and I chatted after Anna left. He seemed a nice, intelligent man and I liked what I heard about the comprehensive detoxification program. I was eager to detox further, go deeper.

I underestimated the man and the programme. Dr A was a ruthless, ego-stripping assassin, concerned solely with the evolution of my soul. It would take two months after the experience before I could speak, and another six months to recover fully. I booked myself onto Dr A's detoxification programme, walking into my next experience like a lamb to the slaughter.

10

In the Hands of a Bitter Man

The day before the fast at Dr A's clinic, I flew to Bangkok, where I was to join Mark at dinner with friends. The taxi pulled up outside The Miami, "A stylish 70's themed hotel," said Mark. I gave the taxi driver the address again, Soi 13 Bangkok. But this seedy place was it. An ancient vase with plastic flowers displayed on an old car radiator dispelled my image of vast white spaces, funky red sofas and a jukebox. "Hi Doll Face!" Mark grinned as I reluctantly checked in, thinking that I should have flown straight to Chiang Mai. A cheerful Mark insisted, "Doll face, one day we will laugh about this!" I winced at the interior design disasters that abounded in the long, dismal and winding corridors. To make up for the lack of marble basins and white, percale cotton, Mark treated me to dinner at one of the best Greek restaurants I have ever eaten at. I broke my diet of juices, greens and salads, to indulge in the delicious bread, *humus* and cooked foods. If I had known how long it would be before I ate again, I would have had more to eat.

After a fitful night's sleep we flew to Chiang Mai in the morning. Dr A and his nursing assistant, Noy, were at the airport in his huge 4x4, ready to take us on our trek into the Thai bush.

Stopping at a Thai restaurant *en route*, I wondered aloud if I could have a little salad. Dr A looked at me disdainfully, asking me why I was so attached to food. My tummy grumbled as I ordered a carrot juice in the vain hope of redeeming myself. I brightened at his suggestion of a Thai steam, then wondered, as I changed in the rickety wooden hut, whether this was an opportunity for him to physically assess me, identifying my weak spots. It was as though he was rummaging in my mind and probing at my soul, but I brushed this off with as nervous nonsense. My constant chatter failed to engage him, the light feminine had no effect on his cool, Samurai demeanour. In the dark steam room I wondered why on earth I had attracted Dr A into my life. My abdomen grumbled, a mixture of hunger and fear.

The resort was in the middle of nowhere, luxurious, remote and with an armed guard at the gate. As I settled into my room I realized that I was the only patient in a facility that could occupy over a hundred and fifty. The detoxification programme was to begin the next day, when I woke. I closed my eyes that night in complete ignorance that I would never be the same again.

 In Brief: The daily protocol was as follows:

- A negative ion generator treatment, my feet in an aqua bath to leach out toxins;
- An infra red ozone treatment;

- Vaginal ozone treatment;
- Rectal/colonic ozone treatment (one warm herbal colema followed by a cooler ozonated water colema);
- Homeopathic detoxification pills and a clear broth soup accompanied the morning session;
- CoRe Energetix reading with Dr A to determine the specific homeopathic treatments to support that day's shedding of emotional and physical toxicity; this was also a counselling and reprogramming session;
- Heat treatment (bath or steam) followed by body work at a local Thai spa.
- Rest (sleep or a movie);
- Vaginal douching with herbs followed by two more colemas;
- Medication, before bed, included Potentised Homeopathic Flower Essences, Antioxidant supplements, Enzymes, Probiotic and Colloidal Silver;
- And not to leave my bum out, a rectal detoxification suppository.

I was sleepy, in my pyjamas, as Noy and a helper set up the room. I had called her at 06:00, when I woke, and I was introduced to the morning round of treatments. The foot bath was frothy and brown within minutes of the machine beginning its bleeping; I coughed violently from a leak in the ozone tent, struggling for air; was startled at the farting sounds during the vaginal ozone treatment; cried with the pain of the deep cramping as the ozone filled my colon; and finally rushing to the toilet. This was fitted with a sieve to catch the excrement, the contents of which was happily snapped by Noy with a digital camera, "Very good," she said, showing me the picture which would enable Dr A to monitor the release of the toxic material from my intestines. Fascinated, looking at my body waste in a new light, I was pleased at this promising release. This was, I thought, why I was here!

> *In Brief:* Dark, toxic material *(mucoid plaque)* resides in the intestines of most human beings. A lifetime of food, emotions and toxic waste is glued to the walls of the intestines, prohibiting nutrient uptake and slowly poisoning the body.

The colemas were not new to me and I had grown to appreciate the release, the feeling of letting go. I created a ritual, lighting candles and meditating on what I needed to let go of as the warm herbal water flowed into me. I visualised the cleansing, consciously released that which did not serve me.

Nervously waiting for my first daily "in session" appointment with Dr A, on the shores of a small lake in the middle of the resort, I wondered how to calm my nerves and steady myself. Perhaps a little spiritual jingle, some kind of mantra, anything in Sanskrit or Hindi, would do the trick? Legs crossed, hands on knees, thumb joined to index finger – I had no idea what the *mudra* meant, but it would impress Dr A with my spiritual being-ness if he saw me – head phones on, I selected a suitable tune and pressed play. An unfamiliar song began to play, the chorus striking a chord:

Say goodbye to the world
You thought you lived in

Take a bow
Play the part
Of a lonely lonely heart
Say goodbye to the world you thought you lived in
To the world you thought you lived in.

Was this a joke, I wondered, suddenly cold, flooded with fear and nausea. I felt as if the Universe or the Gods or something was speaking directly to me, through the immediately available medium. In this instance my iPod. I began the song again. If it was a message then maybe I needed to hear all of it.

In any other world
You could tell the difference
And let it all unfurl
Into broken remnants
Smile like you mean it
And let yourself let go
'Cos its all in the hands
Of a bitter bitter of man

Say goodbye to the world
You thought you lived in
Take a bow
Play the part
Of a lonely lonely heart

Say goodbye to the world
You thought you lived in
To the world you thought you lived in

I tried to live alone
But lonely is so lonely, alone
So human as I am
I had to give up my defences

So I smiled and tried to mean it
To let myself let go.

Was this how it was going to be: Things were going to get tricky; I was going into the unknown; and, if the song was right, "at the hands of a bitter bitter man." Sweet Lord, I prayed, surely this was not my good Doctor!

Dr A's office was a lovely, glass-walled room surrounded by lush vegetation. A table top, fixed to a large rectangle sunk into the middle of the room, displayed a strange machine, a laptop, two probes, a huge crystal and some homeopathic bottles. I liked sitting on the floor, feet dangling into the hole, elbows table high.

Dr A smirked when I told him about my message from my Angels via my iPod. I was irritated when he answered his cell phone in the middle of my story. This was my time, my money! My blood boiled as I listened to one end of the conversation, trying (probably unsuccessfully) to hide my start when I heard the phrase "was it 'demonoid'?" Did demons actually exist, I wondered, hoping that I would never come into contact with one if they did. Dr A did not illuminate the conversation and I will never know whether it was genuine or if it was a ruse to unsettle me.

Dr A used the equipment on the table to analyse my progress, giving me specific remedies to take based on the day's readings. I returned to my room with potions to calm and a crystal to comfort. After herbal tablets and warm broth I was ready for the body work.

Dr A drove to the rustic bush facility, explaining that each bodywork session would be preceded by a heat treatment, alternating hot herbal steam with a hot herbal bath. Clad in a sarong I was led to a steam cubicle, with Dr A demonstrating the controls. The steam room was extremely hot, but I soon learnt to overcome the discomfort, finding a clean sarong when I was done. No sooner was I done, than Dr A mysteriously appeared to introduce me to an elderly Thai woman, Nan, with the face and presence of an angel, who was to be my masseuse. Her hands magically helped my body to regenerate and I felt comfortable in her presence. At first I struggled to relax, panicking at the thought of trying to lie still for the two hour massage. Ten minutes after we had begun a distant radio was switched on, two minutes later I was irritated, insisting that the Thai radio (which I correctly assumed was in the reception area) be turned off. How was I supposed to get in touch with my emotions with that racket going on? After five minutes silence the radio was turned back on, the volume higher. How disrespectful, how utterly rude! "Please get someone to turn the bloody thing off," I said. As Nan shouted through the mesh walls of my room, I spun into a frenzy. How could I do this important work of evolving with these foreign people shouting and making a noise? Ten minutes later the radio was turned off. It took me another half an hour to calm down, only to be thrown into another frenzy at the heavy footsteps pounding down the corridor, neon light flooding the room. Was there to be no privacy, no solace? "Turn the fucking lights off!" I shouted, Nan jumped, yelled and the lights went off, but by the time the session was over I was ready to punch someone. "Did you hear that fucking radio?" I angrily asked Dr A. "Nope," he says. I fumed on the trip back, Dr A spoke about controlling emotions. How the hell was I to do that with all the interruptions? The real work had begun.

Instead of a drink and snacks, Noy waited for me in my room with her tranquil smile, bloody vegetable broth and freaking cucumber juice. I became angrier when I discovered that the vaginal douche was not to be a private affair as Noy had to stay to assist. I was seething inside. I slammed the door behind Noy as I prepared for the colema, ramming the tube up my bum. I could not endure another day like this, everyone was upsetting me, the noise unacceptable. I cried and cried and cried. I just wanted peace and fucking quiet, I howled, praying for peace, peace and quiet, tears running down my face, mucous pouring from my nose, mouth drooling and medicated water gushing out of my arse. Not a pretty sight.

> *Insight:* I thought that I was praying for external
> peace and quiet, when it was internal tranquillity
> that I craved, release from my own destructive
> thoughts and subsequent dramas. I would only
> realise this later during my processing with Dr A.

After the colema I lay, shattered and broken, on the bed, surveying the tray full of little shot glasses filled with specially concocted medications. I drank them all, taking the suppository Noy handed me. I had survived my first day. I would leave in the morning, I vowed. This whole thing was ridiculous and very expensive.

11

The Agony and the Excrement

Day Two

Forgot that I was leaving. Summoned Noy and the day's programme began, a repeat of the previous day but the bodywork session with Nan was unaccompanied by either radio or lights. On the drive back to the resort, Dr A revealed that he specialized in alien abductions. Unaccountably gripped by fear, I wondered what the hell I was doing in this place with this man.

Day Three

Pondering the mirror theory, the theory that suggested that I create my reality. Resting on a bed in the middle of Northern Thailand, I thought I was having the biggest adventure on the planet because I was adventurous. I had found my working environment stressful because internally I was stressed. When my life was boring it was because I was bored. I was loved because I was loving. I was not a product of my environment, rather my environment was a product of me. This meant that if I changed "me" sufficiently, the direct result would be a change in my external circumstances. How to do this?

A timely answer was supplied when I watched the movie *What the Bleep do we know?* It was simple: Change your thoughts, consciously create your life and believe in your power to change your world. If I focused on something long enough it would become solid. If I constantly thought stressful, negative and disparaging thoughts, those things would manifest in my life. Excited at my breakthrough, I felt like cracking open the champagne. Instead, consumed cucumber juice and broth water. During my bodywork with Nan, I felt movement inside my body, hearing a loud popping sound in my stomach. I was certain that the day's photographic evidence would provide impressive proof of the day's releasing.

 Insight: I once viewed new age, metaphysical concepts as nonsensical, if not downright wacky. Now I found some truth that made sense to me, a cataclysmic breakthrough. The Genie had appeared shouting, "Wakey-wakey Gracie, you have been asleep for too long!"

Returning to Noy for "sexy time" (as we referred to the vaginal douching) I found similarities between this woman and a midwife as I received her assistance with my process. What was being born was my consciousness.

That night I was the creator.

Days 4–6
Experience of dumping a lifetime of physical, emotional and metaphysical poisons intensified. Dr A steadily, sometimes forcefully, always relentlessly guiding me towards awakening. My mind running at full speed accompanied by a constant stream of questions, rantings and verbalisation.

Until Dr A slammed his hand on down on the desk, body stiff, his face contorted. Slowly, with clear and venomous intent, he said, "It's as if you have monkeys in your brain," pausing, staring at me intently, "feverishly masturbating," another long pause, "without lubricant!" I gulped, grappling with the imagery. He roared, "SHUT THE FUCK UP, until you have something, anything, of importance to say!"

Yes, he was a cruel and heartless beast, but through the tears of self pity the notion emerged that I did not listen. I was too busy talking; too busy formulating an appropriately witty and intelligent response; too busy focussing on my story; too busy being more important than the other. Self pity became sorrow. Ashamed, diminished, clutching the day's crystal and potions I stumbled to my room. I had nothing of importance to say.

Insight: My mind, always in control, rambling and insensitive, had exhausted me for the past 33 years. The Samurai Dr A had stabbed where it hurt most, not only leaving me reeling for days, but unable to communicate properly for the next four months.

Later, on the way back from the body work session with Dr A, I was silent, angry, offended, unable to stem the tears. Dabbing at my face with a tissue, I reached into my bag for the essential oils that I carried. I smelt them, connecting to the fragrance, dotting the oil over my throat and wrists. I breathed in deeply, centering myself, calming myself, fully accepting the truth in what had been revealed.

"Honey, that is the first time I have seen you healthily self-sooth. I'm proud of you."

It was the only time that he called me "Honey".

Insight: This was first time (in this lifetime) that
I had been able to lovingly offer myself comfort
in a situation where I felt wronged, hurt and
disrespected. I realised that I could not control the
words, deeds and actions of others. I could only
control my own feelings.

Day 7

A gap opened in my psyche, a space created, and the information that Dr A was giving me about how our world is
run began to filter into the fibre of my being. I was horrified when it dawned on me how naive and trusting I had
been, my new awareness creating confusion.

In Brief: The darkness on Earth uses two
mechanisms to stay in control: distraction and fear.
I was distracted from my true nature by television,
by news stories that fed my fear. My mind was
programmed to believe that I was a mortgage slave
who needed a boob job and weight watchers. I was
distracted by the schooling system and religion into
believing I needed to strive to be bigger, better and
more. I was distracted with the belief that I was not
good, never would be good enough, and that God
was external.

I was being programmed to believe that the
enemy was a different race, a different colour, a
different belief system, a different religion. I was
also programmed to believe if I deviated from the
"Successful" life of big cars, expensive homes and
designer clothes I would be a "failure" This deeply

instilled fear kept me in a 9-5 job, preventing me from journeying inwards.

Fear can also be instilled through unorthodox means. Humans are electromagnetic beings, who can be manipulated into states of fear through electromagnetic exposure. We are also affected by the stream of toxins and poisons that are constantly released into the atmosphere.

I asked myself questions: Why are so many American adults on drugs which numb their human nature? Why are people who speak out in truth mysteriously killed? Why is the truth about our alien friends kept from us? Why are people deemed crazy and drugged when they are in the throes of a spiritual awakening? Why does medicine treat only the physical when we are largely emotional and spiritual beings? Why are our children vaccinated and what was really in the vaccines? We have the resources, technology and brain power to feed, clothe and school every person on the planet so why are children in India living off rubbish dumps?

I had had flashbacks of past lives, saw myself as a witch, condemned and killed for my powers. I was outraged at the injustice, at the destruction of the Mother, the Goddess energy. Yet I was a co-creator of all that had been.

 Insight: If everyone on the planet were to realize how powerful, beautiful and light they are, the world as we know it would change in the beat of a human heart. Wars would end, soldiers becoming incapable of killing their brothers and sisters. Camaraderie, support and love would overflow into communities everywhere. The father archetype would provide and protect; the mother would nurture, respected for her intuitive and creative awesome power, revered as giver of life.

My visions left me speechless.

My ego was not in charge, the veil parted and my life was spread out around me in a split second that was also a lifetime. In this timeless place I saw the profound hurt and pain I had caused others; the hurt that I had caused the planet; the sadness that existed; the suffering humans undergo; the shame and guilt in our collective unconscious; and the searing pain of evolution. It was overwhelming.

The most profound experience was the sense that I was far larger than the human life I was living, I was the creator of my existence. I had chosen my family, my upbringing, the events, people and experiences in my life. I was not a random occurrence, a by-product of an evening of too much wine and sex. I had to be exactly where I was and every moment I had experienced led to the moment I was in.

This moment was crushing and hugely powerful. I was perfectly imperfect, in every moment.

Exhausted, I was helped back to my room, aching for the familiar, for food, for my mum, for something I could hold onto. Nothing came and I feared that I was losing my mind.

I woke to flashing lights, a crashing headache and called Noy in panic. She came quickly, clutching vials of medicine for me to drink. Clutching at my sanity, soothed by Noy, I finally slept again.

Day 8

I reluctantly set off with Dr A for the bodywork session, a dark cloud hanging over me, silent, negativity pouring from me. I felt a surge of darkness leave me as I focussed my gaze at a huge palm tree as we passed it in the parking lot. I heard a cracking noise as the twenty foot tree crashed to the ground, barely missing the car. I looked first at the tree, then at Dr A. I had something of importance to say. "Sorry about that." Slamming the door closed, stifling a giggle as I went inside. It was dark when I was done, and I could not resist a quick look at the tree as we sped off. My mind still and peaceful, I stared at the beautiful night sky, noticing the full moon, the stars and the bush.

Dr A said he had something to say. "I hope it's important," I said. Ignoring my sarcasm, he continued, "Grace, while you were having your bodywork, I got the botanists to inspect the tree. They found no rot and no pathology in the roots of the tree. It was a young and healthy tree, there were no discernible environmental factors that caused the tree to fall, no wind or lightening." Maybe it was an attempted alien abduction gone wrong, I thought, but kept it to myself.

"Grace, you made the tree fall." I was silent.

"Yesterday and today you have shed decades, no centuries, worth of dark energy. The Universe wanted to show you what can occur on the planet when that happens." I responded with a non-committal grunt.

Maybe, all over the world, we were making each other sick with our thoughts.

If what Dr A said was true (that my dark energy, thrown at the tree, had caused it to fall) then humans have the ability to make other humans and animals sick with their anger, jealousy, rage, apathy, envy, greed and hate. If this was true then our personal electromagnetic field around us had the ability to create physical changes around us. And if we exuded dark energy the physical manifestations would be destructive. I assumed that this was equally so for light emotions like love, happiness, joy and peace. I thought of London, and the millions and millions of people in that densely populated area, all anxious, frightened, scared, envious and greedy. I thought of the number of times that I had boarded the underground, trapped in a small tin train, deep in the bowels of the earth, absorbing huge amounts of negative energy. No wonder I had gone mad.

That night I stared at my toothbrush long and hard, waiting for it to slide across the bathroom table with the force of my newly discovered powers. The brush did not budge.

Day 9

I woke, powerful, the creator, the master of my existence and destiny. If I held a thought for long enough it would become solid. As within, so without. Thinking about this, I found myself on a rollercoaster of awakening, one minute joyful and high, the next dark and hopeless. But I was kept safe, safe from the pain of cracking open and losing my mind forever. After an uneventful morning, I stepped into a steaming bath, fragrant with the addition of herbs and mixtures, in preparation for the bodywork with Nan. Suddenly I felt ill, the water became an alchemical soup and began sobbing. I wailed, "I'm so sorry, I'm so sorry, I'm so sorry, I'm so sorry," slipping into another world, another time, another land.

Noy, never far away, pulled me from the water. I sat on the side of the bath delirious with grief, remorse, horror, a strange liquid pouring off my skin. Something nameless, bigger than me, was leeching from my pores, and I was grateful that I had no conscious memory of what it was. I slipped back into the bath, regaining consciousness much later back in a small, humble, familiar room.

I was naked, the crickets chirped and the warm Thai night air blew through me. Nan pounded hot, oily, herbal compresses into my body. I felt as though I were in two places at the same time and, as I drifted between worlds, I experienced the presence of The Mother, almost unbearably beautiful and powerful, encircling me, embracing my soul, whispering, "You are forgiven. I have forgiven you." I danced with the divine, an extraordinary moment in the lifetime of my soul where forgiveness and compassion expressed as a physical sensation. It took my breath away, I could not speak, weeping tears of joy as Nan soothed, nurtured and pacified me. Forgiveness vibrated through my body. My slate was clean.

Day 10

I felt a new lightness and freedom as I submitted to the morning round of cleanses. During the rest period I selected some music, Deva Premal and Miten, sitting in a meditative position on my bed as the chants and mantras began. Suddenly all fell silent and dark, my heart pounding in fright. I looked up, gasping. I was the pinnacle of a vortex of angels, a spiral of thousands of shimmering, glowing, angels above my head. Basking in their light, their bright light against a dark, pitch dark sky, I heard someone calling my name, "Grace, Grace!" There was no-one at the door. "Grace!" There was no-one in the bathroom. The disembodied voice belonged to no human being. Exhausted, I fell into a deep sleep.

Day 12
I was beginning to tire of the punishing regime, floating through the day to sexy time with Noy. Naked, crouching, I stared as a large, bright red drop of blood hit the bottom of the bath, followed by another. My moon had arrived, but the blood looked healthy and vital. I called to Noy, who seemed pleased with the colour and consistency. I felt nubile, fertile, delighted with this experience.

> *In Brief:* For years my menstrual blood was dark, thick, almost black and stringy. My regular male doctor and gynaecologist viewed this as normal, but now I knew differently. It was only normal in the light of the toxic load and stress that I carried.

"So, how's your flow?" asked Dr A, as I bounded in for my session.

"I have no idea, but if you ask my tampon, maybe it would be more informative," I quipped.

"The tampon is not designed for the human body," he spat, looking for all the world like an alien.

"Well, neither is it designed as a jet engine," I remarked, unsure what he meant. Angrily, he elaborated, "Tampons stop your natural flow. They are bleached with highly toxic substances and cause diseases that you could not even comprehend!" There was more: "Not only do they dry you out, they do not degrade and only an unevolved being would even contemplate its use. Evolved women use little pieces of cloth that they wash and have one to two drops of blood." This sounded gross. My ego, hurt, interpreted this as being called unevolved. I sent him a third eye message, telling him I thought he was cruel and unkind, but could not say it out loud.

If Samurai Warrior was so agitated, though, there must be something to what he had said. This guy knew his stuff. Even though I was upset, still ruled by my emotions, I resolved to think the matter over.

 In Brief: I was to hear the same views, and more, in Tantra School later. There I was to learn about womanhood from an ancient, sacred and highly revered perspective. I was later grateful to this man who had cared enough about my health to penetrate what can sometimes be a very thick skull. I have not used a tampon from the day that I learnt about the dangers from Dr A.

Day 14
I was done. This was my final day.

I bid a tearful farewell to Nan, my bodywork angel, bowing deeply and reverently to this wise teacher and healer.

"I have wiped you clean, whatever you decide to fill your head with from now on is who you will become, make your choices wisely." His words cautionary, sending a shiver through me. As he revealed his plans for me, I was chilled to the bone. No bubble bath, no comfort, no good food.

12

Temple Tantrum

Dr A thought it was a good idea that I enter a local Buddhist Temple where I would meditate for 10 hours a day, in silence. I thought this was a terrible idea. He also told me to continue fasting. Another terrible idea. He told me I might be expected to shave my head. At the impending loss of my bleached locks, the symbol of my femininity, I wept. Dr A chastised me for holding onto my vanity at the expense of the evolution of my soul. I pictured my new life as an emaciated, bald, celibate, hungry and silent nun.

Yet, wildly and unreasonably (probably from starvation) I told my landlord that I would not be returning to Samui. The die cast, I really was living out of a suitcase, feeling as though I had fallen off the grid. I felt incredibly vulnerable and truly at the mercy of the Universe. Perhaps I would shave my head and live in a cave. I could wear orange and remain silent all day, since I clearly had nothing of importance to say.

I paid the substantial bill and said my goodbyes to Noy. Brother Mark arrived at Dr A's, finding me considerably thinner and quieter. Dr A and Mark drove me into town to buy temple clothes. Anything baggy and white. As I registered at the Buddhist Temple, I was greeted by a surly little Thai Monk, who explained the rules and gave me a key to my room. I had no idea what I was doing there or what I was to do next.

Outside, in the sunlight, I looked at Mark, my heart filling with warmth and love. As I gazed at him, he appeared to change shape, becoming older, taller, looking like my father. Open-mouthed, I blinked, hard, but there he was, my father, looking back at me.

Insight: This was one of many experiences of shape-shifting. My mind grappled with the fact that my father was in Britain, so could not possibly be outside the Buddhist Temple, getting in the way of this mystical moment. This skill, the ability to see into the human hologram, was frightening to begin with, but I have learned to breathe through it.

My room at the Buddhist Temple was spartan, cold, tiled, furnished only with a wooden slatted bed with no mattress. There was a cold shower and a hole in the ground for a toilet. I slung my bags onto the wooden slats and sank to the floor.

When the lunch bell rang I entered the food hall, finding everyone present dressed in white, staring at the floor, neither talking nor making eye contact. Ignoring the buffet stands, one marked "normal", the other "vegetarian", I headed for the tea stand and poured hot water into a mug. After fourteen expensive days of ridding myself of every toxin known to man, I was not about to pollute my system with MSG, salt and soya sauce. If Jesus could do 40 days so could I. Two meals were served daily, breakfast and lunch, with no-one eating after 13:00.

Meditation began, for me, after lunch. I had to complete 10 hours a day, in silence, alone. That's an awful long time for me to be with myself. Timers were provided which hung around our necks so that we could alternate a 15 minute sitting meditation with 15 minutes of painfully slow walking meditation. And so on and so on. At night time we were allowed to speak to the residing monk. A queue of Western spiritual seekers lined up outside the door. When my name was called I entered the room on my knees, bowed to the Buddha statute, both hands on my third eye, heart then floor; then I would bow to the next person, third eye, heart, floor. There was a lot of bowing and scraping. I was allowed a couple of minutes with a beautifully kind and compassionate monk. I invariably had little to say, probably because I had not eaten in about 18 days, nevertheless I felt comforted by his presence. After my evening session with the monk I went back to my chilly room, washing with cold water. I fell asleep crying.

After seven days, I needed to get away. I could not cope with the isolation, craving love and the company of people who cared about me. I could not stare at the bleeper that hung around my neck any longer. I was hungry and a little crazy. I had to get back to Samui. But the Temple gates were locked, there was a leaving process and only the head monk could grant permission to leave.

I called Dr A. I needed to escape, I told him unemotionally, on medical grounds. I wanted to continue my cleanse and dedicate time to a further 7 day fast at the Spa, I continued, showing the face of a detached Samurai Warrior. I would have to speak to the head monk that night, he said, and if I was granted an honourable discharge, I would be picked up and could spend the night at a local guest house. I packed my bags immediately, talking my way out of the Temple, in amongst much bowing and scraping. But not before attending a leaving ceremony which were held twice a week. I was in luck, there was one that evening. Thank the Pope, I thought. Dragging my bag down from my room, there was no one to say goodbye to because I was not allowed to speak. I sort of nodded but most people were walking around slowly staring at the floor, wall, tree or the sky. I almost sprinted to the gate, spotted a familiar 4x4 and leapt into it. Noy greeted me with a knowing smile. I was driven to a delightful guesthouse, where I ran a hot bath and crawled into a bed, with sheets, a mattress and a duvet. I was grateful for this luxury. The room even had a flush toilet, I felt like I was in heaven.

I arrived in Samui on Christmas day, checked into a hotel and went straight into another 7-day fast at the Spa. After 21 days of not eating, it was easy to continue, and I was still getting rid of very old toxins from my gut.

My psychic abilities were on the rise as I continued fasting. I began to see images and predict events.

One evening, whilst eye gazing with a male friend, I was startled to see his skin peeling away, fangs growing from his mouth while his eyes increased dramatically in size. He was shape-shifting before my panic-stricken eyes. Bile rose into my mouth, I quickly stood up, walked around, and when I returned he looked as he usually did. I told him what I had seen. "Cool," he said, "Do do you want me to do it again?"

"Sure," I replied. And he did.

Insight: In dim light people would morph,
becoming animals, or changing sexes, or shifting
into ancient beings. I started to see differently, my
ability to do this the result of shedding 33 years
of vaccines, environmental pollution, toxins I
had acquired from everyday food and water and
electromagnetic bombardment.

Visiting Mark one night, I made my way along the familiar
path to his shack, the ocean stretching out before me. In
the dark I began climbing the stairs to the porch, stepping
up and suddenly out into space. It felt as though I shot
out of my body, into the universe, finding myself floating,
looking down at Earth and the other planets in our galaxy.
Bathed in divine light, floating in conscious energy, I was
filled with the divine life force that is creation. All is One.
This knowing was in my bones and blood, psyche and soul.
In a microsecond, one mystical moment, a grand cosmic
truth was shown, transforming my being until the end of
time.

I stepped onto the next step, then the last, staring into
the shack, with a sense of timelessness. There was no time.
What the fuck just happened here, I wondered, as Mark
rushed by me.

"Are you OK?" he asked.

"I think I may be God."

"Gotta pump the toilet, Doll," he chuckled, leaping off
the porch and into the night.

Insight: From that moment no human face
ever looked the same. I saw me in everyone and

everyone in me. Words cannot explain the force,
the power and the majesty of that experience.

After 30 days I broke my fast with a fruit platter. I stared at
the fresh papaya, banana and mango, spearing a piece of
mango with a cake fork. Holding it up close so that I could
see the intricate fibrous texture, I smelt it, finally biting
down. The juice and sweetness exploded in my mouth, the
luscious nectar running down my throat. I thought I might
die from the pleasure of this exquisite fruit. I chewed and
swallowed, taking my time, closing my eyes as I orgasmi-
cally savoured each morsel of my delicious ritual meal.

My friend, Anna, was moving to Ubud in Bali, and I
decided to join her. I needed to retreat, wanted peace and
quiet. Incapable of holding a conversation, recovering from
the physical, mental and spiritual shock of transformation,
extreme cleansing and fasting. I said goodbye to Samui,
jetting out on the same flight as Anna.

13

Standing at a queue for passport control, I was nervous as my one-year Thai visa had been obtained by unorthodox means. I suddenly felt dreadfully ill, falling to my knees, breaking into a sweat, my hands clammy. Something tugged at my neck, the pendant and chain that I wore clattering as I fell to the floor. I tried to steady myself, my face and hands ice-cold. I scanned the area around me in a fruitless attempt to see who had ripped my necklace off. Pale and sweating I approached the unsmiling passport officer, who stamped my passport and moved me along. I collapsed into Anna's arms, clutching my pendant (a flower of life design) and the chain, which had no visible breaks. "My angel, when you move from the darkness into the light, there are forces that do not want to see you go. They will try and scare you and take things from you that represent the light. To the extent that you have been dark, will be the extent that you will be light." We boarded the near empty flight to Bali without further incident. Travelling with Anna was an experience of blankets, raw chocolate, pillows, cushions and lavender eye masks. I soon feel asleep.

From Dempasar we travelled to Ubud in a beat-up car, dirty, full of boxes, a puppy, recycling and items that had to be dropped off *en route*. I would grow accustomed to the dreadlocks, armpit hair, tattoos and strange amulets, crystals and bracelets that adorned these new acquaintances. In my life as a city girl I would have viewed these "people" as dirty, crazy, good-for-nothing hippies. How wrong I had been in my judgement. They seemed kind, giving, loving. They had a way of disconcertingly holding my gaze, smiling, as if drinking me in. Ubud was place of deep ravines, plants and bushes covered in fine tumbling fern, hidden houses and distant fires. I was introduced to Bali Buddha, a delightful raw foodie, organic type of place that suited my preference for juices, smoothies and salad, which I chewed thoroughly.

Anna and I checked into a beautiful hotel which was to be our home while we looked for a house. It was difficult for me to speak, Anna shielding me from the unconsciousness energy that affected me deeply. That afternoon I experienced pain in my body which exhausted me. I fell asleep the instant I hit the bed, waking 18 hours later, still fully clothed.

At breakfast I ate my fruit slowly and mindfully, but could not ignore the American couple nearby, their table groaning with food. Eggs, bacons, sausage, toast, butter, jam, tea, coffee, pastries, and fruit, it seemed enough for a family of eight. They were both large, with their abundant flesh hanging over the sides of their chairs. They did not speak to each other, exhibited no joy, no gratitude for the meal they were eating, nor did they seem to appreciate each other's company. They ate like programmed robots, shovelling food in, barely chewing. I hated them, loathing their unconsciousness and the way that they reminded me of what I had been. Anna rescued me, holding me as I wept uncontrollably, the couple oblivious to my breakdown. "Just love them," Anna said, helping me to my room and a soothing bath, "You have immense power in your human heart, don't fuel the hurt, just love them, my Angel."

I slept a lot in the next few days, which passed in a blur. I often saw flashing lights and experienced painful splitting headaches.

Insight: The flashing lights, something like lightning, and the headaches were to last a few months, probably the result of my pineal gland kicking back into life after 33 years of calcification, connected me to the spirit realms. My neural networks and pathways were being rewired as I found a new way of perceiving and being in this world.

When Anna took me to inspect the enormous house that she had found for us, I could barely see it past the lush forest garden. Pushing open the wooden gate, I crossed the wooden bridge over a small stream and pond, approaching the three-storied fairytale house. The kitchen was an open space with wrought iron filigree decorations in window frames, no doors or glass. A huge queen-sized day bed stood outside the kitchen in a large, white and open room (which may have been a lounge), at the opposite end of which was the entrance to my bedroom. This was a large sunken room, separated by glass from the magical forest outside and painted a dark green. Twists and turns led to an enormous spa bath, enclosed by beautiful stained glass windows and doors, which opened in turn to an outside shower with ivy-lined walls. It was spectacular. Anna's room had a separate entrance and was above the white room, far enough away for privacy, but close enough for safety.

We prepared to move in several days later, finding the house still dirty and without the promised beds. Anna made a call, and ten minutes later, Wayan arrived with deep apologies. Ceremony had prevented them from cleaning up, as promised. In Balinese culture everything stopped for ceremony or temple, nothing took precedence.

On hands and knees, cleaning, I discovered a pond outside our kitchen area. About the size of a table, it was overgrown with moss and various water plants. A tiny pair of black fish lips broke the surface of the green water, nibbling at something then disappearing again. I tugged at the mossy debris, revealing a shy, black fish hiding in a corner. Delighted, I showed Anna our new house mate. "I feel his name is Dodo." Anna said, "So be it, Dodo it is." And that is how my friendship with Dodo began. While he cowered in the corner, I promised him yummy fish food, also not to hug him, because if I took him out of the water he would die.

Anna found a driver, also named Wayan. She hired a cleaner, also called Wayan, the name given to every firstborn child. The second born was named Kadek, the third Nyoman and the fourth Ketut. Anna spent her days designing her vibrational range of yoga wear, working in a factory with many Wayans and Ketut's. I spent my time with Dodo dressed in *her* clothing, covered with sacred geometric symbols, silently moving around the house. But I was not alone.

I was being watched, I could sense movement, that there were other entities in my environment. I began to relate power outages and light surges to my moods and internal shifts. I was connected to the weather, especially storms, my body cocreating with Mother Nature. Anna smiled at this. "Do you not know that you are a white witch?" I was horrified. Witches cackled, rode on broom sticks and had huge noses with warts; they were scary, even evil. Under Anna's steady gaze, my mind opened to a new idea: I had no idea what a witch was, only what I had been told. Perhaps I had been lied to by people afraid of the supernatural feminine power of witches, kept from discovering my own power and connection to all.

 In Brief: My religion had told me I was a sinner, I should fear the wrath of God, worship only his son, Jesus. But I believed only in the power of love and interconnectedness of all things. I believed in kindness and I believed that my breath connected me to my spirit. In the moment I believed this I was infinitely more powerful than the stories my upbringing had told me. I was connected to God, I was God, she was me and I was it, and everyone else was a reflection of God. God was not a white man nailed to a cross, this was a mad message. He was our divine messenger our Godlike reflector. Man and humanity used a misinterpreted message to suppress the human race, we were bound by the shackles of religion, it was disempowering the world.

The only true message was one of love and compassion, nothing else. Anna was witness to this, my psych breaking free of dogma and the suppression of my innate, loving and intuitive feminine nature. If thinking like this made me a witch, I was glad to be one!

She made me a special tea and we sat outside under the moonlight. She spoke to me of protection, as Dr A had done, warning that when one opened to the light, the darkness would try to keep them as source of power. The power that I gave was my anger, anxiety, greed, envy – the dark and heavy emotions that I had constantly given – these fed the dark energies. "Stop feeding them," Dr A had said, "but once you break free they will not let you go lightly." Anna and I exchanged thoughts, confirming his prediction. As white fear swept through me, I recognised that I was in a dangerous period. Anna calmed me energetically in a timeless space, before reminding me of the experience at the airport, telling me that I needed to protect myself.

 In Brief: I was becoming multi-sensory, developing the ability use psychic and telepathic forms of communication. Between Anna and I words were insufficient. Language seemed a limiting communication.

Apart from sleeping tethered to Anna's body, how was I to protect myself? My dreams were real and lucid, but I could not control these states and their outcomes. Anna sensed my panic, soothing, *"My angel, my heart, love is your protection."*

This was insane, I needed spells, a broom stick, a cauldron, a fancy cloak, eye of newt and toe of frog. I needed a black cat. I worked myself into a frenzy, lightening flashed around me, and I could tell a storm was brewing!

"My heart, it's a clear night," said Anna.

Insight: It was a new experience, the "I" watching "my" mind freaking out!

O, boy! Anna followed me to my room, lighting candle after candle. "All of the beings and entities that exist in realms other than this, whether light or dark, need love. We need not fight them, we withhold our judgement. We offer only love," she said, sitting on the edge of my bed. I opened my eyes wider in fright when she told me that, according to Balinese cultural beliefs, we were not suitably protected as the house was in the unfavourable position of being "above the temple line"; and the Bali Spirit was notoriously angry and fearsome.

"You have a visitor," said Anna. "Where?" I asked, looking towards the door. She pointed, "Look, she is there". I gasped at the fairy which sat on my left leg, a fairy of purple and pink light with a beautiful cherub face. "You can see her?" Anna nodded, adding, "She is giving you a gift, what is it?" The tiny being placed a wand in my lap. I said excitely, "It's a wand, Anna!" She smiled, kissing me good night. I fell asleep clutching my fairy wand.

Grace!

I woke, startled, sitting up in the four poster bed, draped with white net. The garden beyond the glass wall was alive in the gusty wind, with hostile creatures hidden beneath the flapping undergrowth. I heard an animal panting. It sounded large, cat-like. In the dim moonlight, through the white netting, I saw an enormous, jet black jaguar. It

paced, yellow eyes gleaming, breathing hard. I closed my
eyes, opened them again. It was still there, with enormous
fangs, looking hungry, but with a quality of animation, it's
pelt almost too shiny. Where the fuck was the fairy and the
bloody wand it had left me? I scrabbled under my duvet
cover and on the bed, no luck. Dreaming or awake, my
reality was in this moment. Anna would kick this jaguar's
butt, but I had no way of rousing her.

Other animals approached the room, closing in, waiting
to pounce, waiting for me to give in. Through the curtain
I watched as the jaguar paced restlessly, angrily. Sweating,
I remembered Anna's words, "Love is your protection."
Attacking the jaguar with a pillow and an incense stick was
not going to work, so love was all I had, but how to invoke
it? It came to me, William's prayer for protection, a gift
from the past. Breathing deeply I chanted, "I am the light,
I serve the light, I love the light, I love myself, I love God, I
am one with God." Pausing, I peeped through the curtains.
The jaguar was still there. "I am the light, I serve the light,
I love the light, I love myself, I love God, I am one with
God. I am the light, I serve the light, I love the light, I love
myself, I love God, I am one with God!" I repeated it until
love poured through me and out of me, I became pure
love, innocent love, divine love. When I looked around,
my darkened room was empty. I sighed in relief and joy.
Love really was my protection.

I opened my eyes and it was morning, sun streaming
into my room, the familiar noises of bikes and cars filtering
through the air. I had survived and I was alive! I felt as
though I had woken from battle, my body sore and stiff.
Getting out of bed, I carefully put both feet on the ground,
resting a moment. In the middle of my room were three

huge paw prints. No prints leading to them or from them. Inspecting them, I could clearly see the print of the inner pad, the paw toes and the nails, each paw print double the size of my palm. Was the black jaguar my shadow self, my alter ego, my "id"? If so, had I made peace with this frightening, dark side? Or was this Jaguar Medicine, with its shamanic associations of reclaiming power, shape shifting, psychic vision, facilitating soul work and a symbol of gate keeping to the unknown? Perhaps, as the Mayans believe, this Jaguar was a dangerous sorcerer, or a powerful spirit guide, or even calling me to a healing path?

I had no answers, and perhaps these black shadows were the dark side. What a ride! I looked at myself in the mirror. Only one thing to do. Tell Dodo.

I had breakfast with my fish. I was eating fruit, he was eating fish food. I recanted my story of the jaguar, unashamedly embellished, wanting to impress him. His fish lips rose to the surface in praise of my bravery, I am sure.

14

Saved by an Avatar

Days became weeks, weeks rolled on into months. I rarely left the property, sleeping, reading, practising yoga, while Wayan the driver drove Anna, Wayan the cleaner busied himself around the house. "You live very much up there," said Anna, pointing at her head, "you should be more down here." Pointing at her heart. "You need help."

Heavens, not a daily 10-hour head stand pose mediation!

"Marijuana," said Anna. In spite of my frightening experience with *Iboga*, in spite of the strict drug laws and harsh punishments around Marijuana use, we ditched Wayan the driver and set off for Ubud. The 2-hour drive would be a piece of cake, I said, until I saw the road map, which lacked basic components such as road names, direction markers, junction numbers and popular landmarks. In short, it barely qualified as a map, looking like a photograph of spaghetti which someone had thrown all over a floor. It was like trying to get directions from studying a plate of *fettuccine al fredo*. I threw it in the bin, relying on intuition for direction. Zooming happily along the Balinese highways, we drove into a town, where, I said, we would be pulled over by 3 policemen, who would smile and let us go. Anna did not like that idea, but at a traffic light a Balinese policemen waved us down. You have taken a wrong turn, he said, but not to worry since Rp3 000 000 (£200) would see us back on the road again. Anna and I looked at each other. "Why do you want to take our money," she asked, leaning across me. He grinned, Anna blinked her large blue eyes. He smiled, slapped the car and told us to go, being careful not to take any more wrong turns.

 Insight: Had I predicted or created this? I knew only that my thoughts and external events were inextricably linked.

The trip was successfully concluded using my own intuitive navigation system. We purchased our "supplies" before driving back to Ubud on the spaghetti highway.

I nervously prepared for the mind relaxation process, tapping and releasing using the EFT that I had been taught. I ate raw chocolate filled with a mixture of the herb, fried in coconut oil. My experience was gentle, of loving, expanded energy. I felt into myself and my "beingness", wonderful, funny and beautiful. Why was this feeling illegal in our toxic world, where alcohol and pharmaceutical medicine were not? Perhaps it really was a conspiracy to stop people from feeling their power, from being mellow, loving and laughing. I felt connection and warmth, watching animal spirits dancing in the trees above me.

 Insight: I was in a higher vibratory field, where I could see that which was not available in the very

narrow band of visible light that the human eye
could discern.

Laughing, I ran a bath, opening the stained glass windows
to a night sky peppered brightly with brilliant stars. Sipping
Guinness and carefully puffing a clove cigarette, I gazed
from my naked body to the heavens, Michael Buble playing
softly in the background. God, I felt like a woman! What
a beautiful plant what a beautiful feeling why should it be
a heinous crime to smoke a little naturally growing plant
and feel great... connected to moon and stars I allowed the
warmth to envelope me, in gratitude for this moment.

Dodo was a great listener. I would talk to him about the
movies that I watched in case he was interested in sacred
geometry, remote viewing, Buddhism, Melchezedek, the art
of dying or ecstatic birthing. I was absorbing more material
to discuss with Dodo, when I heard Anna calling, "Angel!
I found something, come quickly!" I unravelled the paper
towel in her hands to reveal a little bony creature, covered
in a sack of hairless skin. It had enormous ears and eyes
and the body of a rat, or maybe a tiny cat, or perhaps a bird.
I was unsure if we should roast it or rescue it. Anna had
settled for the latter, it had already been seen (and injected)
by the local veterinarian, Wayan the driver transferring cat
litter, food, milk and a blanket from the car. We called it
Avatar, and gave it a little milk to drink. This androgynous
and strangely mystical creature pooped everywhere and
was so tiny I thought I would crush it or lose it. It slept on
my heart when I lay outside in the sun. We made a bed
from towels with a tiny pillow which we laid at the bottom
of a brown paper bag. Placing Avatar in this cosy bed, it told

me, "I am going to die tonight." I returned it's gaze, "You go whenever you feel ready, you are loved."

I slept well that night, an indescribably deep, restorative and nourishing sleep. The next morning the Avatar's makeshift bed was gone. With tears streaming down her face, Anna sat before an object covered with a cloth bearing a purple and golden Tibetan symbol of eternity. The majestically covered bundle was surrounded by seven burning sticks of incense and a thick scattering of petals. After three days with us, Avatar had died.

Together we cried, mourning and honouring the life of the little creature. Anna broke our meditative silence asking, "How did you sleep?"

"The best sleep ever."

"Me too. Grace, this was a real avatar! It took something dark from this house."

With the aid of Anna's compass, we found a suitable burial site at the bottom of the garden. Anna dug the hole while I reverently carried the body of Avatar from the house, still draped in the purple and gold cloth.

"How big should the hole be?" Anna asked.

"A hole big enough for a croissant," I said, weighing the little bundle in my hands.

And then we laughed, me holding the stiff kitty-mouse-bat-angel and she hanging on to a spoon turned spade. We completed our ceremony in gratitude for each other, our temporary visitor and for laughter.

Feeling strong enough to hire a motor bike, I rode around Ubud, stopping in at an internet café to let my long suffering mother know that I was indeed alive and well. From the air conditioned cafe, which smelt of plastic cables, I watched a Balinese funeral procession as it passed by. It was a colourful affair, with people singing as they walked the coffin through the streets. Unlike western funerals, this was a beautiful celebration of life. I stared at the coffin as it was borne into my line of vision. "Won't be funny if the coffin fell over," I thought, then watched in horror as the coffin started to do just that. The men carrying it grappled to stabilize it, but managed to hoist it back onto their shoulders. The procession continued but they looked a little shaken. I was a little shaken. I needed to be more careful with my thoughts!

Back in our magical house I began preparing the afternoon meal, noticing that I was working with a blunt knife. And I wanted oranges. Instead of toppling coffins, I could try using telepathy for something useful. I would send a message to Anna to bring back a strong sharp knife and four oranges. The energy parcel that I sent focussed on two words: knife and orange. But then I thought that she might return with an orange knife, so I concentrated thought on pictures, and sent those instead.

Anna returned with bags from our local supermarket. I waited patiently as she unpacked, revealing a new knife. I was delighted. But when the bags were empty there were no oranges. Disappointed, I told her about the telepathic message. "Oh, Angel" she smiled, "I don't eat oranges, but was drawn to the citrus section where I stared at the oranges for a while, I really did not know why!"

15

Pharmageddon

Lounging on the sofa, enjoying a raw chocolate ball, I thought about my doctor back in Oxfordshire. "So, Doc, I see flashing lights, have painful headaches, I talk to animals and they talk back; I can make objects move with energy, I believe in aliens, see angels and the odd demon; I have witnessed evil; sometimes I feel the pain and sadness of the entire world and wish that I could live on another planet with kind and evolved beings and never have to speak to another human again." I laughed, maybe I would go and see him, to watch him wriggle and ask how my bowel movements are! I was sure he would order an immediate blood test, or a battery of tests, and he may wonder if what I had was viral. When the tests failed to reveal abnormalities, he would refer me to a specialist who would, in turn, diagnose me as a bi-polar manic depressive with suicidal tendencies and possible social anxiety disorder. Whatever it was called, it could be managed by a regimen of medication. I would swallow pills for months on end, only to become really ill as the (often devastating) side effects kicked in.

I doubted, very much, if any practitioner that I had met would tell me that I was having a spiritual awakening, and that physical symptoms were the result of shedding emotional toxins.

How many lives were ruined by horrid little pills because medical science did not understand the nature of *dis-ease*? How had I been affected by the prescription medication that I consumed for years?

 In Brief: The relatively new science of medicine dispensed with the wisdom of ancient practices of yoga, homeopathy, chi gung, Chinese medicine and plant medicines, but failed to develop remedies for many modern illnesses. The solution, I was to learn, could not be found at the same level of consciousness as the problem.

I was living an idyllic life filled with raw chocolate, yoga and sunshine. I woke when my body wanted to, had no schedule to keep, I did not need to set an alarm. What an appropriate word for that object that wakes up so many people. Alarm. Also meaning panic, fright and anxiety. While the water heated up on the stove in a glass pot, I lit a stick of incense, grabbed the fish food and went to visit Dodo. He guzzled away while I informed him that he was my research partner, that we were doing an investigation on prescription drugs. Since he lacked opposable thumbs, I told him I would do the internet research.

I had taken a popular antidepressant for years. When I started taking the medication I weighed 60 kg. By the time I found myself at the endocrinologist's office a couple of years later, I weighed in at 110 kg. I was also a nervous wreck, anxious, had nightmares and battled to sleep; I struggled to concentrate, felt isolated and thought I was going bonkers; I did not have a relationship with a man because I had no sex drive and I suffered from severe pain that seemed to come from deep in my bones.

A reliable source listed the common side effects of this popular anti-depressant as: abnormal dreams; anxiety; decreased sexual desire or ability; diarrhoea; dizziness; drowsiness; dry mouth; flu-like symptoms (e.g. fever, chills, muscle aches); flushing; increased sweating; loss of appetite; nausea; nervousness; runny nose; sore throat; stomach upset; trouble sleeping; weakness; yawning.

My symptoms were the common side effects of the drug that I was taking. There was another list, the *severe* side effects. Out of a very long list, I had experienced these: tightness in the chest; bizarre behaviour; confusion; decreased concentration; fast or irregular heartbeat; fever, hallucinations; new or worsening agitation; panic attacks; aggressiveness; impulsiveness; irritability; hostility; exaggerated feeling of well-being; seizures; severe or persistent anxiety; trouble sleeping; suicidal thoughts or attempts; tremor; trouble urinating; unusual bruising or bleeding; unusual or severe mental or mood changes; unusual worsening of depression; and last, but by no means least, weight gain. It became all too clear how these "magic pills" had fuelled my ill health

I wondered how many times doctors had stunted or completely halted spiritual awakening in their patients. Powerful drugs numbing the very unfolding that was a completely natural process of evolution. Psychiatric practice in general could be said to ignore the magnificence of the human spirit. It had kept me small and disconnected, fuelling my separation and invoking insanity in its truest form. Insanity in the form of total isolation from my soul and the souls of others. I let it all sink it. Phew.

My time in Bali was drawing to a close, but I did not want to go back to Samui. I needed something to tackle, something to work through; I needed love and a partner but there was still something unresolved within me. "My angel, my heart, you need Tantra," pronounced Anna, "there is a school in Thailand. Go there, my heart, and learn. It will change you, it will give you something." As long as "something" was not a sexually transmitted disease. Tantra School. It sounded perfect.

I bade farewell to Bali and the house that had held me, visiting Avatar's grave to give thanks for his protection. I said goodbye to Dodo, thanking him for his company, although the conversation was always one-sided. I thanked the Marijuana for it's lessons and for being part of my journey, not feeling the need to ever use it again.

There were no goodbyes for Anna, my sister forever. I thanked her for wisdom, guidance and love. The taxi driver, Wayan, whisked me off to the airport, stopping only at Bali Buddha for supplies. I bounced into the airport wearing Anna's yoga wear, boarding my flight to Bangkok.

At Suvarnabhumi Airport, Bangkok, I headed straight for my favourite juice bar, Squeeze, ordering a "Pretty Lady". Smoothie in hand, I hopped into a taxi to take me to my hotel. I loved the drive from the airport into Bangkok, it was hot and the familiar skyline made me feel at home. I checked into my four star hotel with its cool white sheets and marble bathroom. Under the harsh lights I could see that I needed to get my hair done before the flight to Samui.

There was a salon in tuk-tuk distance of the hotel, with a hairdresser who spoke little English and had a severe facial tick. But I was not put off by this. Holding up my blonde hair, I pointed to the roots saying, "same same, but not different." He smiled knowingly and I assumed that he had understood. Thirty minutes and a rinse later I was wheeled back to the seat in front of the mirror. My hair was grey with a green tinge, but became greener as he blow dried it. I was silent, but mad as a snake, struggling not to become hysterical. When he was done, I pulled at my hair, my voice rising as I asked, "What happen, I no ask for GREEN!" By now the hairdresser knew that he had messed up. He did not want to lose face and, in typical Thai style, began yelling at me, "You leave, you leave, you go." In case I did not understand him, he pointed wildly to the door, "YOU NO PAY, NO PAY, YOU GO NOW."

In Thailand the customer is always wrong.

16

The Unassisted Orgasm

Back in Samui, I headed straight for my reliable L'Oreal hairdresser. "What happen?" Toe exclaimed, surveying my bright green hair.

"One night in Bangkok!"

"We fix, we fix," laughed Toe.

I resolved to accept the results, whatever the outcome.

Insight: When I was able to accept a situation as it truly was, my internal world improved dramatically. Conversely, I created much internal suffering when I could not accept my outer circumstances. My ability to cope with change was growing.

In Brief: The process of change can be seen as various stages which people experience, illustrated by the human change curve. The stages are shock, denial, blame, confusion and resistance. Once we push through resistance we move into the positive emotions of acceptance, testing, exploration and finally integration. My first reaction to my green

hair the day before, was one of shock. Denial
was expressed by the thought that this could not
be happening, quickly shifting into blaming the
hairdresser for the mess. Then I blamed myself for
going to him in the first place, becoming confused,
wondering how it was possible for someone to
dye another persons' hair green. I fell into total
resistance to the horrible colour that clashed
horribly with my beautiful tan and the image I
wanted to project. A few minutes later, realising
that this man was not able to fix it, I accepted the
result and his earnest invitation to leave. Letting go,
I began to embrace the green hair in the knowledge
that all would be well.

I left the salon a luxurious brunette, embracing my new
dark tones and embarking on a shopping spree. This was
not the same as shopping on Oxford Street, London, a
sophisticated whirl of glittering decor, tiled floors, enticing
window displays, goods carefully presented and impecca-
bly groomed sales ladies dressed entirely in black. Samui
offered something altogether different. Many shops opened
only at lunchtime, closing late in the evening. My favourite
store, opposite Siam Commercial Bank, was an overstuffed
room with a mezzanine level where the store owner's two
children slept. I would know when the children were in
as Ay (a common name in Thailand) would ask me to
whisper quietly and not to talk on the phone. Dresses and
clothes covered every available surface of the dishevelled
home store, some displayed on hangers suspended from a
mesh framework which ran from floor to ceiling. When I
found something that I liked, Ay would eagerly rummage

through large plastic bags piled up in a corner, in the toilet or upstairs in his bedroom. Finding the dress, he would hang it in the large, cylindrical frame, covered with a flimsy curtain, that served as a changing room. Inside this cramped frame, I would awkwardly wrestle with straps and arm holes of the dress that Ay passed me. When it was on, I would emerge to Ay's shrieks of delight. "Look beautiful, look beautiful look belly belly beautiful", he would exclaim excitedly, his enthusiasm completely unaffected by how I actually looked in a particular dress. I soon found that these "one size fits all" ensembles did not always fit me. The average Thai woman is the size of a western pre-pubescent teenager, so European sizes 10-12 were considered large. Sometimes the "store" girls would giggle when I asked for my size, responding loudly, "No have your size, too big, too big." Ay's place was a safe bet for a woman, and I could rely on finding a few right-sized items there without hugely denting my confidence. A couple of strappy, long, polyester Thai dresses in hand, we haggled over price, agreeing when I felt I was getting a bargain and Ay was happy with his profit. I needed this man, who stocked my size clothes, to remain open for business. In mutual agreement THB1500 (£25) was exchanged for several items. Feeling like a million bucks I left Ay's store wearing one of my new dresses.

Before setting off I carefully tucked the long dress between my legs, not wishing to be choked to death by clothing caught in the wheels of a 50cc motorbike. With my new brunette hair and new Goddess dress blowing in the wind, I turned my thoughts to the important task of preparing for Tantra school. I had three weeks on Samui before I embarked on Tantra One, and I needed a lover to get limbered up for all the sex stuff I was to engage in. Jacko was cute, well built, on a spiritual journey and a man of science (a dentist). From New Zealand, he worked with Mark on a detoxification process (well connected) and stayed in a bungalow opposite mine. Jacko and I swam, ate, laughed and joked, fast becoming friends, but he was shy and I hesitated to approach him about sex.

There was to be no need for a direct approach, our growing closeness unfolding in an entirely natural way. We sat, one day, on his bed which overlooked the ocean, talking about love and past relationships. There was little for me to reveal, but Jacko moved closer to sit on the windowsill as he spoke about his last girlfriend. He had been in his car in a parking lot, she had ended the relationship over the phone. After the call, he told me, he experienced chest pains and his world went silent. "Grace, I heard a tearing noise, like someone tearing a piece of paper in two, I struggled for breath, thinking I was having a heart attack, it literally tore me apart." He paused, tears in his eyes, a halo of sun behind his head. He continued, speaking slowly, "I know I have scars on my heart, no one can see them, but I know they are there." Gazing into each other's eyes, it felt as though I was processing his pain. My heart opened, tears streamed down my face. We connected somewhere beyond the pain, feeling into each other, our minds in perfect synchronicity.

"Will you make love to me?"

"Yes," he replied simply, sending my heart leaping and my body buzzing with anticipation.

My bungalow, a beautiful air-conditioned villa with one bedroom and a stone bathroom, was the perfect setting for an evening of love. When Jacko arrived preparations were complete: candles in all the corners of the bedroom, four candles around the bed (which had white percale cotton sheets), soft, white rosebud fairy lights adorning the head-board; the room cleansed, lighting incense I blessed the space; and dressed in white, was waiting when he arrived.

"Are you ready for me?" he asked, moving towards me, up close. He smelt fresh, his skin warm and I giggled in response to his playfulness. His touch delicious, he stroked my skin, ran his fingers over my cheek; then kissing, long, wet kisses, his tongue probing my mouth gently; hands sliding down my awakening body and between my legs, I was wet and wanting. Slowly he undressed me, garment by garment, before disrobing himself. I watched in delight as his truly impressive penis stood at attention (I silently thanked the Universe for hearing my first prayer). Desire coursed through me as I stared at his firm, wide, member. His manly salute ready to serve. My hot liquid essence was desperately and eagerly awaiting penetration. As he plunged into me, taking my breath away, I trembled in ecstasy.

 Insight: We were both, at that time, goal oriented, driven by the need to orgasm. In the past I was rarely able to relinquish my power and open myself to allowing a man to bring me to orgasm.

Jacko moved above and inside me, pleasuring me, loving my body. Suddenly, unexpectedly, I felt the rising of energy from the base of my spine, the warmth spreading up and outwards. Gasping in surprise, I wondered, could I be having an orgasm? Waves of sensation crashed over me and I clutched the sheets on either side of my body, a visible sign of reluctance to let go. Then I orgasmed, grabbing the sheets tightly, head thrashing from side to side. I cried, "I don't know what to do, I don't know what to do, I don't know what to do!"

"O, ye of little faith," said Jacko, gazing into my eyes, not faltering, riding me steadily, me riding the waves, finally climaxing with me.

I was not sure if this was tantra but it was a damn good start.

Insight: I had been given a gift of surrender. I felt honoured by this man who offered his total presence and connection.

As we lay together in the magical glow of the candles, I become conscious that Jacko had never once looked at my vagina. He had briefly touched her but almost seemed afraid of her. I intuitively felt that he was disconnected from the feminine. I kissed him lovingly.

Insight: The vagina, or sacred flower as I love to call her, is the essence of the feminine. Jacko had been hurt by the feminine and this created a disconnection, an imbalance, in his life.

"Jacko, I sense you have been wounded in the past by a woman. I would like to perform a ritual if you agree, to help you to reconnect."

He looked at me, fresh from the shower, naked. He smiled, nodding his head. We made ourselves comfortable, he at the foot of the bed. "You are to gaze at me, connect with my feminine power." I lay back, propping myself up with pillows.

Even with the sense of sacredness of this act, I prayed my flower was pretty enough, good enough, pleasing to his eye.

I quietened my mind, connected with a deep sense of knowing, then slowly, with a sense of purpose, I opened my legs. Jacko stared intently at the part of me that was deeply feminine. I watched him as he gazed at me.

Minutes passed. His face became angry, his brow furrowed as he seemed to be engaging in telepathic dialogue with my vagina. With a single focus, not looking anywhere else, he moved in, searching, closer. Face contorted in pain, tears in his eyes, he remained motionless, a gentle dance of energy between us. He softened, then, tears flowing, and I opened to his courage. Sensing a shift, I whispered, "Would you like to touch her?" He nodded. "Jacko, touch her gently and mindfully, touch her just as you would a delicate flower." His touch was slow, almost pensive, curiously childlike and innocent at this introduction, this discovery of the feminine, the loving mother, the all powerful beauty of creation. In reverence for me and for all womanhood, he said, "You have a beautiful flower." The ritual was complete, humbled by the experience I felt that I had been in service.

Insight: I did not know at the time that this was an ancient, sacred ritual called "Yoni Gazing." *Yoni* a term used for the vagina.

"Why now, not a week ago," I asked, curious about the timing of our intimacy.

"I wanted to make love to you when I saw your vulner-ability. I saw it when you cried with me and asked me to make love to you from your feminine space."

The remaining days in Samui were blissful, with my friends regaling me with unfounded rumours of Tantra School. It was allegedly a place of black magic and dark energy; Swami was purportedly strange. But then such a place, and the person who ran it, was bound to be contro-versial. I was not deterred, happily setting off for one week of loving.

17

Tantra: The Sacred Shag

Tantra School was on another island in the Gulf of Thailand. Substantial, the various campuses scattered over the island and divided into halls, it could accommodate up to 200 students with a complement of 50 teachers at a time. Besides Tantra, the school offered numerous courses – paranormal psychology, heart meditation retreats, the art of dying, complete femininity, yogic healing and metaphysical yoga to name but a few – and Kundalini yoga. In London I had heard that kundalini yoga, when performed properly could drive the practitioner mad. The notion intrigued me.

> *In Brief:* Kundalini is a powerful energy that lies at the base of the spine in the form of a coiled serpent. Some believe that activation of this forceful and potent energy was enough to cause insanity when the serpent reached the third eye. Of course I was drawn to this mystical insanity.

After registering, I dumped my bags in bungalow, heading out for dinner at the Yoga Café on a hired bike. Sitting alone at a wooden table, looking out over the dark ocean, I wondered if I would have to get naked and orgasm in front of a hundred people. I stopped my mind in its tracks, refusing to attach a story to my feelings of loneliness. I was not going to worry about the future, nor was I going to judge my emotions

The bed in my bungalow did not have white sheets, which dismayed me greatly, and they were a polycotton blend. Horrified when I saw that the sheets were not clean, I solved the problem by spreading a towel over them.

The next morning I carefully dressed in (colour co-ordinated) clothing (suitable for yoga) before I bounded down the steps of the bungalow, eager for my introduction to the mystical art of tantra. Expertly kick-starting the motorbike, I waited for the machine to roar into life. It did not, there was a weak splutter from the engine. I jumped on the starter kick stand thingie again, opening the throttle. Still nothing. I tried again, and again, jumping up and down in maniacal attempts to kick start the bike.

"Oh for fucks sake, fucking bike," I exclaimed, noticing my neighbour before I could curb myself from swearing.

"Obviously you have very little energy in your *manipura* chakra."

What on earth was he talking about? The bike was buggered and I was late for my date with Tantra! Head shaven, gaunt, clad in white fisherman pants, a Tantra School shirt with "Teacher" on the back, he glided calmly down the stairs. What sort of teacher? Perhaps he was my key to my sexual healing and would become my new sex guru. He asked me to dismount.

"I hope you mean the bike," I said cheekily with a wink. He did not seem amused. "I've flooded it, for certain, or it's a dud," I rattled on as he gave it a single good kick, the engine revving into life.

"No energy in your *Manipura* chakra," he said, patting me on the solar plexus.

I had, it seemed, nothing of importance to say apart from thank you, and rode off to Shakti Hall, gears crunching.

There seemed to be a thousand other bikes in the parking lot. The check-in desk was manned by an Adonis, muscles bulging, a flowing mane of dark hair. He was hot, which I thought would be an asset with this business of Tantra.

> *Insight:* Many of the men at Tantra school were sexually attractive, and for that I will be eternally thankful. But my judgments were false. Good looks do not equate to great tantra.

Textbook in hand, I found a space next to a woman who I thought must be the oldest person in the room. She glowed, her blonde hair wild and her blue eyes shining. I thought she was brave, doing Tantra 1 at her age.

Jayne was in her 50's (I thought she was 10 years younger) and was to become a friend, ally and one of the many spiritual partners I would connect with. I was still introverted after my experience with Dr A, mindful about how much I spoke. I did not feel like connecting with everyone and I would choose my friends wisely.

Not wishing to introduce myself or chat, I busied myself with centering, waiting for Swami to arrive. Of course I had Googled this chap, not content entirely with Anna's recommendation. An unattractive Eastern European, he had founded one amongst a handful of international tantric yoga schools, and he was late.

At 10:30, an hour and a half after the official starting time, the big guy crashed through the double doors at the back, striding heavily up the length of the hall. Silence descended as the hulking figure, clothed in orange, walked up the stairs of the raised platform. Tucking his feet underneath him, he placed a pillow on his enormous stomach and positioned his arms on top of it. His demeanour proclaimed his status as Top Dog, Alpha Male. I would not have been surprised if he had urinated on the pillars, marking his territory.

"Welcome to Tttuuunntra!" His voice loud, resonant, holding onto consonants and vowels, rolling them out in an Eastern European accent, he continued, "This is a step by step course on Tttuuuuunnntrikyoga, especially in its sexual aspects. It is based on the ancient tantric texts recorded in India, Kashmir and Tibet." He surveyed the hall, "You must have a serious attitude towards Tttuuuunntra, this is not a license for FORNICATION," his voice rising, "nor is it about lukewarm romanticism. Nor is it a platform for," he paused, "Rudeness," flicking his sweaty dark fringe from his face.

"Tttuuuunntra is an accurate science of personal development, which will confront you with fundamental questions about your life, about man, and about the Universe." This guy was not joking, he was passionate with a capital Pee!

"Fuck Us," he roared.

I gulped, who was *Us* and was *fuck* a word even allowed in this school?

"Fuck us," he repeated, "fuckuss carefully on what you do." Relieved, I understood, listening carefully. "Be open to transform and understand, if you do not fuckuss the results will be scarce and your time here will be lost time, because then you will never understand what Tttuuuuunnntra is."

The student pool had, I was sure, been skimmed of those hoping for a casual shag. "May this course be profitable to all those who want to join the beauty and pleasure of an erotic life within the depths of spirituality," he pronounced. Amen, Brother!

Swami explained the difference between the right and left hand paths of tantra. Most Westerners, being gross of spirit, would be incapable of following the high and abstract path of the right hand. Tantra of the left was a suggested starting point for us, as it was more down to earth and included the physical act of sex act in its practice.

In Brief: The right hand path of tantra contained much symbolism, a path for ascetics without the need for physical union. The highest form of tantra, it was a search for a divine union with a deity, or an incarnation of the divine, sometimes through supernatural beings. Although sexual in nature these encounters are a sublime and spiritual way of interacting with the source of pure love. It was also the worship of the ten great cosmic powers within certain Tantra schools.

Swami warned us that moralists and amateur outsiders consider Tantra as a horrifying heresy, a spiritual deviation, connected it with smut, fornication and black magic. The left hand of tantra was viewed with scepticism by the, "Narrow Minded Ones and the Sexuality Frustrated". He spoke of sexual frustration as the highest crime that a human could commit. "The left hand of Tttuuunntra is not practiced for the sake of sex itself it is an instrument to go beyond sex. It is a tool used to reach health, balance, improved relationships, self control and supernatural states of consciousness." His voice rising, "This would CULMINATE IN STATES OF PURE CONSCIOUSNESS OF *SAMADHI* THAT IS TTTUUUNNTRA!" I wanted to scream, breathe god-damn it, BREATHE!

At last Swami inhaled sharply, flicking back his fringe, seamlessly continuing his impassioned discourse, now on the differences between red and white tantra. Red tantra was mainly practiced in the West, it was tantra for pleasure, tantra for a deep connection to another being, it was a form of conscious sexuality. Swami's dismissal of Red tantra had me questioning what I thought I knew about the path.

 Insight: During my time in London I thought that tantra could show a different way of having sex, something more profound than the meaningless bumping together of genitals with its fleeting goal of ejaculatory bliss. The Tantric courses that I attended struck the heart of sex and pleasure, addressing the wounding and the feelings of guilt and shame we hold around our genitals. I began the process of erasing old belief systems around the sacred act of sex. I began to reclaim my sexual power, allowed myself to feel pleasure, and to choose who I shared my body with. This early work through Red Tantra, shallow as it seemed through Swami's eyes, was nevertheless a valuable introduction, and probably all I could cope with at the time.

White Tantra was practiced at the school. A body centred spirituality, it was a way of going through the world of nature and matter in order to experience divine consciousness. "Tttuuunntra," said Swami loudly, "is the cult of the feminine." It was a form of Goddess worship, it was accessible to anyone regardless of caste, creed, gender or social status. "Tttuuunntra DOES NOT EXCLUDE."

Intellectual knowledge of the non-dualistic nature of Tantra, understanding of its metaphysical premises, was not enough. "In Tttuuunntra there is an absolute need for a personal experience accessible only though Shakti, the divine feminine principle." Tantra sees and reveres the female body as a beautiful instrument and an unavoidable premise for spiritual realization. At times Swami spoke without pauses in a continuous, relentless stream, channelling from the place where truth lives. I reacted emotionally, experiencing conflicting anger, sadness and helplessness as I remembered past pain. His words stirred up memories of being taught to hide my body, vagina and breasts hidden, never spoken of. Systematically disconnected from my own female sexuality, Mummy June was only able to approach the subject of femininity once, when she felt obliged to deliver The Menstruation Talk. This was accompanied by a diagram of the uterus, fallopian tubes and vaginal canal, drawn in a black marker on the kitchen table, while she "explained things" to me. I saw how programming and disempowerment began with babies, with their little hands smacked, a sharp, "No," when they naturally discovered their genitals. Flushed, uncomfortable with the thoughts that rose to the surface, I listened to Swami talk passionately and eloquently about Tantra. It seemed to be the most natural and stunningly beautiful practice one could express through a human body.

A music meditation followed, during which we were instructed to simply allow the music to penetrate us fully, to feel whatever response and emotions moved through us. The meditation focussed on the second chakra, the *svadistana* chakra, responsible for sexual energy, desire and emotions. The music started, I felt energy move in my body as I sat bolt upright, legs crossed, hands on the back of my knees. There was a sudden searing pain in my belly, the pain of past, anger towards my mother and grandmother for not being wise enough, for passing on a destructive chastity mentality. Momentarily caught off guard by the intensity of the emotion, I allowed myself to explore. Going through it I found more, I discovered my rage, outrage that my own earth mother had failed to teach me how to be a woman in the most basic and fundamental ways. Was this not her role? Was this not her job? She had chosen a constrictive religion and a patriarchal stance over her daughter's flowering sexuality, she was a weak and pathetic mother. Seething in righteous judgment, I heard a small voice struggling to be heard over the hurt and rage. Breathing, quiet, allowing the fiery emotion to die down, I listened. "Grace, your mother did the best she could. She broke the mould of her mother's destructive beliefs so you could break yours. This is the path of evolution, the path of the great unfolding. You will break your mould so others can break theirs. And on and on it goes. Everything is and was in perfect harmony and perfect order."

I was not an isolated particle of pain. I was the wave of evolution. I was a part of the Goddess unfolding. These concepts did not exist outside of me, I *was* the concept. The music ended and I opened my eyes, my yoga top drenched in tears.

Insight: I was, by this time, accustomed to hearing voices. I accepted this ancient wisdom as a revelation from Source, the voice of the feminine archetype.

At 12:30 we broke for lunch, Swami grumbling about running late, majestically descending from the stage. Jayne and I made small talk and I felt a warm connection with her, feeling safe in her presence. The afternoon's yoga instructor wore white, a woman with a nice round belly, glowing, supple and braless. Was that in order to keep the heart area open, I wondered. The Hatha yoga practice was a gentle balance of yin yang energy, preparing our minds and bodies for the meditation and talk to follow.

I enjoyed the music mediation, gratefully contrasting the day's process to ten hours silent meditation. The afternoon's music corresponded with *mulhadara*, the base chakra, where our primal nature resided, responsible for vitality, survival and security.

In Brief: Through connection to the earth this chakra is also the body's energy battery. It is the seat of mysterious kundalini energy and therefore contains the potential for cosmic union.

As the music washed over me and through me, I waited for a resonance, a stirring, but nothing happened. Jayne and I partnered for the discussion after the meditation, sharing what we had (or had not) felt. Her openness in sharing her thoughts and her body experiences put me at ease and gave me permission to be as honest in return.

Swami was half an hour late for the next session, heavily taking up residence on his throne. Without apology for his late entrance, he launched into the topic of relationships.

Citing the Indian Master Bhagwan Shree Rajneesh (aka Osho), there were three alchemical stages to relating. The entry level relationship, symbolised by a square, was the most common. These partnerships consist of two people, plus their projections of what they believe the other to be, with the result that there are four people in the relationship. They do not know who their partner is, nor is there any authentic communication, which may be expressed as, "You are not the man I married", or, "I don't know who you are anymore". The woman falls in love with her own idea about the handsome prince and he, in turn, may have loved his own idea about the sexy princess. In both cases their conceptions of one another have little to do with who the other person really is. So when a person acts in a way that is not congruent with the other's projection, cracks in the relationship appear.

The second level relationship is symbolized by a triangle. The lower two corners of the triangle represent man and woman, the top represents oneness, or unity. This unity is often occasional, experienced during deeply connective love making at which times the couple come together, their usual state being one of felt separation. So this relationship ebbs and flows in and out of unity.

The third level, represented by the circle, is a complete relationship. This is not a relationship we have with another, but rather within ourselves and with the divine. The circle represents perfection, transcending time and space, uniting the two halves of yin and yang. This is a merging with spirituality and divine consciousness, through the awakening of the crown chakra, *sahasrara*.

So this was the goal of tantra: a union with the divine. White tantra offered direct and simple access to all humans – white, black, yellow, homosexual, criminal, thief, farmer, prostitute, sinner or saint – an invitation to merge with God. Such a powerful experiential encounter was bound to rock the taught belief that God was something outside of us, accessible only to the very few, and only through dualistic religion. Perhaps this is why religions were not keen to embrace this ancient and mysterious art form? Maybe this is why tantra was depicted as a smutty, unholy practice? Had established religion conspired to keep secret the truth about these powerful and experiential ways of knowing God? I imagined Dr A would be pleased with my line of thinking as it would fit neatly into his conspiracy approach. Maybe he would consider that I finally had something of importance to say.

Swami left the building after answering questions from admiring students. It was late when I pulled up outside my bungalow, free to digest the teachings of the day. My helpful bald neighbour arrived at the same time, introducing himself as Gabriel. Angel Gabriel, I thought. Tantra school was not what I had expected, visions of orgies in steamy rock pools rapidly receding. It did not look like there was going to be a general swopping of partners amongst a great heaving exchange of sexual energy. It was at once more mundane and extraordinary, seekers on a path of exploration, a journey towards the Divine, learning how to use the instrument of their bodies to get there. I showered, sleeping well, oblivious to what the next day held.

Swami was only forty-five minutes late, without pre-
amble announcing, "The topic of ejaculation". He spoke
frankly, freely without a hint of shame or embarrassment.
I stifled a giggle when a quick glance around showed that
I was the only one finding it funny. In the tradition of the
school, semen and menstrual blood was seen as *Ojas* and
were not to be wasted. Ejaculation for men was strictly
forbidden to conserve the limited amount of *Ojas* that men
were born with.

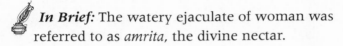 *In Brief:* The watery ejaculate of woman was
referred to as *amrita*, the divine nectar.

Swami believed that when we had used up all our *Ojas*
we would die, exclaiming that teenage boys all around the
world were literally masturbating their lives away. Men
who learned the art of retention could experience internal
orgasm, forcing their powerful energy up through the body
and with training, past the heart, throat, third eye and
eventually the crown chakra. Moving the energy through
those centres would result in mystical, divine and powerful
experiences.

Men at the school had to train for an initial period of 49
days during which they were to make love without ejaculation. Many paled at this excruciating thought (some were
to cry with frustration in the weeks to come).

Swami moved on the topic of the female orgasm, of
which there were five types. "The superficial orgasm," said
Swami dismissively, disdainfully flicking his hand towards
his penis, "is a reflex in the genital rrrregion, down *thehair*."
He bellowed, "It is a mere stimulation of the extra vaginal
erogenous area, especially the clitoris. Is it associated with

a stiffening of the muscle of the thighs and belly with fear, deep psychic tension, an immobility and a rather sad and desperate attempt at reaching an orgasm. It has the sensation of pushing down with a piston, which then quickly discharges. This is almost like a constipation." He was not finished. "It is associated with egoic tendencies and masturbation, and is very frequent nowadays. This orgasm is located only in the genital area and is totally partial and incomplete, leaving behind an unsatisfactory mood and a level of frustration." This was an eloquent and accurate description of my usual experience. Now it had a name, it was a superficial orgasm, a mere reflex. I felt sad, certain that there was more.

I felt deep love for this outwardly fearsome man, gratitude that he had overcome ridicule and persecution to offer his teachings, so that I could listen to him speak with neither embarrassment nor shame about this deeply condition. I raised my hands to my heart in gratitude.

Flicking his fringe back, rearranging the pillow on his stomach, he said, "The deep orgasm is complete and may present paroxysmal manifestations, such as tears, cries, cessation of breathing. Deep undulations spread throughout body. There are ways to induce this state, which we cover later, and it will become apparent to you why, when you reach these higher states of consciousness."

Then he began speaking of the Titanic woman who, when making love, wants the man to ejaculate because she knows that she is killing him slowly with every ejaculation. This woman uses sex as a power play, not caring about orgasms, whether deep or superficial. Something went "ping" in my heart. I had found a deep satisfaction in this way of engaging sexually, particularly with older and powerful men. Swami was talking about me, addressing me directly.

 Insight: I could equate the Titanic woman to the woman in JP's Stage Two relationship model. It was a destructive archetype to embody.

Swami explained that women stored deep hurt in the walls of their vaginas as physical knots, holding tension, emotion and trauma. "Internal massage is the remedy," he said, inserting his middle fingers into an imaginary pipe in front of his face. He explained that there is a specific way to perform this, from the outside spiralling inwards until the cervix is reached, his moving fingers illustrating the technique. When a hard knot or blockage is encountered, gentle circular massaging must be applied until the tension is released. He warned that this release may be accompanied by emotion, hallucinatory visions, flashbacks and sometimes complete loss of consciousness.

Listening to Swami's continued exposition on the different female orgasms, I was distracted by my pressing need to evolve, selecting Swami as the man to facilitate this. But how to reach him? Seekers at my level had to wait four weeks for an appointment with him. That was way too long, my need was urgent. I energetically connected with this man who held the key to my rapid unfolding, determined that it would be as I desired. I formulated a plan and at 12:30 when the lunch bell went I was ready to execute it. At the end of the session students lined up politely, each hoping that their pressing sexual queries would be answered by the big man. Swami would only leave after dealing with the last student in line, either answering their question or quelling their concern. I joined the end of the line, considerately offering others the place before me, thereby making certain that my conversation would not be overheard. As the queue in front of me became shorter, I became increasingly nervous. One of the girls in front of me stepped up to the stage, bowing strangely to Swami before sitting at his feet, gazing at him adoringly, while he patiently responded to her questions. The next student did the same thing, falling at his feet in a worshipful pose. Grow a backbone, ladies, I thought, delivering the girls a lecture in my mind. Did you hear nothing about the celebration of the feminine, the bit where the God worships the Goddess? Treat him with respect, but as an equal in this journey. Then it was my turn.

Heart thudding, I pulled my shoulders back, projecting confidence, asking Swami to please move up as I preferred not to sit on the floor. He stared at me, I thought admiringly, while he cleared a place beside him, saying, "Of course, the only rightful place for a Goddess." Up close I studied him carefully. Physically not my type, nor did I particularly like the way he smelt, but underneath all those orange robes lay the key which would unlock my union with the divine. I beamed, "I need your help".

"Certainly, certainly, you will find the afternoon session very helpful."

This was not the response I had hoped for, so I repeated, "I," placing my hand on my heart, "need your help," drawing a circle with my finger over his genitals. He looked blankly back at me. I took a deep breath and finished with the deal clincher, "Personally". He stared, sizing me up, then asked, "What are you doing at lunch time?"

"Your place or mine?"

"Mine," he said, asking for my mobile number, which I wrote on a piece of paper obtained from one of his devotees. He would contact me after he had eaten. I floated away, pleased with the direction my tantra school experience was taking. I hopped on my bike, kick starting it first time around, scooting off for lunch. Changing in my bungalow, I checked my mobile for a signal every few seconds. As 13:30 became 14:00, I wondered what on earth I was doing here, on a tropical island, about to drop my brooks for an Eastern European Tantra Swami so that he could massage the inside of my vagina with his short thick fingers!

He was a famous (or at least semi-famous) tantric master. My imagination ran wild. No doubt he had a large bedroom, serene, overlooking the ocean, definitely with white linen sheets on the four poster bed, golden curtains billowing in the wind. There would be a bright, sophisticated kitchen, possibly open plan. Certainly an office adjoining his bedroom and maybe a lounge with beautiful, wide sofas and scatter cushions galore. A large, opulent bathroom, mainly of natural stone and if he was a discerning man, a little bit of marble and a shower big enough for three.

My phone beeped, interrupting my reverie. I grabbed the device with sweaty hands, reading: 1 New Message. "My darling Shakti, if you have had lunch and are ready, please come around to mine. Directions to follow." *Ohmygod*! What had I manifested? At least I had a hospital and medical plan to fall back on, and there was a one million baht payout on my demise!

It was a three minute ride east along the coast. With a thudding heart I parked my bike outside his compound and made my way down the makeshift garden path looking out for billowing golden curtains. There were none. But there was a sea view.

The sign outside his house read, "Please leave your shoes outside and ring the bell." This seemed pointless as I could clearly see only one poky room to the left and another to the right, both off a well-used, short and shoe-filled corridor. But I complied, removing my shoes, then rang the bell. Swami had changed into a T-Shirt with the elephant god, Ganesh, printed on it and fisherman pants. An orange Alice band kept the fringe off his face but his hair stuck up like a bizarre peacock's tail. "Come through to my office," he invited, leading past the bedroom (on the left) into the study (on the right). The place was untidy, with files and papers everywhere, thousands of DVD's and a large desk, facing the ocean. He offered me a seat close to his, gazed at me intently, and asked, "Why are you here?"

I cannot remember what I said, what he replied, or how long we sat there before he grabbed my chair, which had wheels, and pulled it closer. Our knees touching, he stared at me intently, then holding my hands he closed his eyes saying, "I want to check your chakras!"

"Yes," I said faintly, "very good idea." Pretending to close my eyes, I kept them slightly open and watched him. "*Muladhara*," he intoned. Bloody hell. Had he had forgotten my name? I almost corrected him, but then remembered that it was the name of a chakra. Relieved, I tried to concentrate, but which one was it? "*Muladhara* is your base chakra," said Swami, reading my mind, "I am going to say the names, *fuckus* on that place in your body until we move up." That sounded easy, moving through the body to the crown!

"*Svadhisthana*," he said, and with a sense of triumph I remembered this one. I had nicknamed it the sex chakra and focused on the area. "*Manipura*." Where had I heard that before? Of course, Angel Gabriel, telling me that I had no energy there because I had not been able to start my bike. This was my solar plexus chakra, related to fire, ego, will and expansion. It was Dr A's fault that it was a limp watery pool, that I was a wet fish. Was my ability to hold a conversation held there as well? I had a sudden urge to call Dr A, tell him I have something important to say and demand my third chakra back! With all my might and will I infused the area of my solar plexus with wrath, fire and brimstone. Taking a deep breath as Swami squeezed my hands, saying that we were done. "Oh," I said, wondering about remaining four chakras.

"Your *Manipura* chakra is weak." News spreads fast, I thought, I would need a bike with a push button start. "So," was all I could say as his face altered and he began rubbing my thighs, first my outer thighs, then the inner thighs. He pulled me even closer, running his hands down my back, massaging, stroking, touching. This must mean I had passed the chakra test. We were in a strange position, almost hugging, and I could see files in the bookshelf behind him, one marked "COSMIC POWERS" standing out. That's what I needed more of, I thought gleefully. But after a few minutes of groping, I felt uncomfortable, like an object. Could he not tell that this was doing nothing for me? "I think you are a dirty old man," I blurted suddenly, pushing my chair back, instantly regretting my outburst.

He only chuckled, "Why don't we go to my bedroom, where it is more comfortable?"

"Sure," I responded, curiosity getting the better of me, almost changing my mind again when I saw the chintz Thai curtains, the anti-clockwise clock, and cheap golden cat with a mechanical paw that went up and down. Clothes lay on the floor and a book of babies' names was next to the bed. His cupboard was a metal shelving unit packed with Swami clothes and towels. The room was small and pokey. Then there was the bed. Not a hint of white linen. It was unmade, the duvet scrunched in a corner, the mattress covered with a patterned, maroon, fitted bottom sheet. I was horrified, a closer inspection revealing that the sheet was not patterned, but stained. Heavily stained. From human fluids. The sheet would be a forensic nightmare. I knew, from the lecture, that the big man did not expel fluids, so I deduced that the excretions were those of satisfied women, scores of satisfied women. The horrible duvet was patterned so it was more difficult to tell if it was also stained.

"Come, my darling Shakti," said Swami, reclining on a pile of pillows like a fat comfortable cat. "Swami, do you ever wash your sheets? They are positively filthy!"

"To be surrounded by the fluids of the divine feminine is beautiful." Oh God, how many days or weeks or months accumulation of fluids? Mummy June would have her washing machine working overtime on this lot. But this was no time to be thinking about my mum. I covered the offending sheets with the duvet, and gingerly lay down next to him. Dwarfed by his body, cuddling, his hands all over me, I wondered if this was tantra. What was I missing? There was no turning back. I had created the situation, and having come this far I wanted freedom, I wanted liberation, I wanted deep orgasms and most of all I wanted to meet God.

In the middle of this little foreplay ritual, a rolling and tussling affair during which I was put off by the copious amounts of facial hair that spiritual men seem to require, I had the notion to shower. I wanted to be super clean and I wanted my vagina smelling like fresh flowers, in case he chose to gobble her up. I struggled free, stopping him in full *mojo*, announcing my intention to use his bathroom. He told me that I was clean and did not need to shower. Angrily I insisted, "It is not your role to tell the Goddess what she wants, Shakti wants to shower, please could I have a *clean* towel."

"Well, if that's what Shakti wants, the clean towels are in the corner."

I moved through the (bitterly disappointing) galley style kitchen to the bathroom. There were dirty dishes in the sink, lunch still in a bowl, fruit lying on the counter and a kitchen floor that looked like it had never seen a wet mop. The bathroom was tiny, the shower head positioned over the toilet and a large bucket in the corner for a Thai style bath. As a trickle of water ran out of the shower, I wondered how I was supposed to meet the divine in a shitty bungalow like this.

Persevering, I walked seductively sashayed back to his room, draped in a small, off-white towel. I found him texting whilst stroking himself. Maybe I was more of a Red tantra girl after all, but the phone disappeared when he saw me. He watched me intently as I let the towel drop to the floor. It was liberating to stand naked in that Thai hut, in the middle of the day, in front of that man. He seemed appreciative, reaching out for me. I crawled provocatively over to him, panther style, and he began touching me, his hands rubbing my body, his fingers expertly running through my hair. He was experienced, and whatever it was he was doing stoked a hidden fire inside me. I had a man who would serve me, who could control his energy and mine. I forgot about sheets, captivated by my own need and his penis, springing into action. His stubbled face skimmed my rounded firm breasts, his breath arousing a pulsating erotic feeling. My nipples stood erect and sensitive as he expertly tongued them. This man was lost in my body, lost in my wanting, he forcefully opened my legs, admiring my pussy, and hurriedly buried his face in her juiciness. He lapped her up, rigorously awakening her. She seemed to waken from numbness, responding slowly to his erotic intentions. I felt we had had enough of the "sex stuff", now I wanted more of the "meeting God" stuff. Sensing my thoughts he said with emphatic desire, "My darling, it takes at least twenty minutes before I can consider entering you. It is vital to warm up The Goddess." So I lay back and allowed. When he felt I was a suitable conduit for moving this powerful, and now cultivated, sexual energy, he entered me skilfully. I was wet and yearning to be penetrated, a deep groan of pleasure escaped my throat.

I felt like I was having a good time, he deftly twirling me, lifting me, flipping me until finally I was on top of him. In an instant I flipped into trance. Life slowed. Suddenly my body was electric and I had dropped out of my mind.

My body began moving from a primal place, a place of deep wanting, a place of the Goddess. My hands rose above my head in what felt like an ancient invocation to the Gods. I circled around his hard masculine, being deeply penetrated in this natural human union. Strange sounds came out of me, Swami below me shunting my energy around and into him. Eventually I stopped moving, receiving all of him inside me, alive and connected. In a space where I could simply *be*. When I emerged from my trance, Swami was still inside me. He took my hands in his as he eased me onto my back. The two of us lay silently in divine togetherness.

Stirring awake, I looked at the clock. So this was why he was always late! Swami let out a deep, wanton groan as I bent over to pick my pants up from the floor. This was just the beginning, he promised.

I sat smugly amongst my fellow students, glowing with my practical and personal introduction to tantra. Swami came in fifteen minutes after me, displaying no sign that we had been romping around together a short while before.

18

The next morning, in a kind, nurturing text message, Swami enquired how I had slept and if I was sore. We agreed to reassess my condition at lunchtime and discuss our next session. Still smiling, I set off on the new bike which required less brute force to start.

Everything in the opened air venue seemed perfect that morning. The hall had a large concrete floor, with a concrete wall behind the stage that the teachers used. Supporting beams ran down the middle of the hall, with three walls of green mesh from ceiling to floor. We sat in rows, our yoga mats demarcating our generous space allocations. I stretched on my mat, enjoying the surroundings, the tropical plants and the incense.

Swami arrived, on time, and I wondered if he had cancelled his early morning trip to heaven because of me. Without a sign of acknowledgment, he began an impassioned speech on the age old topic of size. Notebooks in hand we braced ourselves for the Size Matters talk.

 In Brief: Much of Swami's information on this particular topic is taken from the *Kama Sutra* and the *Ananda Ranga* (an Indian sex manual written in the 16th century).

"Yes, size does matter," said Swami bluntly, "and if a man has a small penis it is due to bad karma". Glancing around the room, it was apparent from their discomfiture that several men had bad karma, the insight prompting me to cross some names off my List of Potentials. Swami continued, telling us that during tantric lovemaking the head of the penis has to touch the cervix. If it does not, powerful cervical orgasms will not occur. I doodled a cervix in my book as he explained the three sizes of the male organ, or lingham, and of the female organ, or yoni.

Men were categorised as Hare, Bull or Stallion. The Hare had a lingham that did not exceed twelve centimetres when fully erect. This man was generally fairly short, well proportioned with a quiet disposition. The quiet, short men in the room began to perspire.

The lingham of the Bull does not exceed eighteen centimetres, the man is robust, with a high forehead, large eyes, a restless temperament and he is always ready to make love. He is known as a man of medium dimension. This type of man sounded crazy, with huge eyes, permanently hungry for sex and restless.

The lingham of a Stallion did not exceed twenty-four centimetres, and, "The owner of such an implement (I stifled a giggle) is usually tall, large-framed, muscular and has a deep voice." Many men nodded knowingly and seriously to one another in the room, until Swami continued with, "He is described as gluttonous, covetous, passionate, reckless and lazy. He walks slowly and cares little for lovemaking." Swami added, "Unless! He is suddenly overcome with desire. His semen is copious and salty. He is known as a man of large dimension."

I wondered if *Kama Sutra* or the *Ananga Ranga* were having a laugh at our expense. None of this lot sounded remotely appealing. I was distressed at the notion of a world full of lazy, slothful men, or ones that were plain crazy. Then it was the turn of the women.

Yoni's were also categorised into three different sizes, the Deer, the Mare and the Elephant. At the last I almost choked on my own saliva. This was going to get ugly. The Deer was described as a vagina not more than twelve centimetres in depth; the woman would have a soft, girlish body with well proportioned breasts and solid hips; she would be a moderate eater and be addicted to the pleasures of lovemaking; and her yoni juice would have the pleasant perfume of lotus flowers. I wondered what a lotus flower smelt like.

The Mare had a yoni that did not exceed eighteen centimetres in depth; she possessed a delicate body with broad hips and breasts; and her umbilical region is raised. I thought that sounded a bit like me, working on the physical description rather than a depth measurement.

The Mare is versatile, graceful and affectionate; likes good living and lots of rest; she has big, beautiful eyes and a long neck; she does not easily orgasm and her yoni juice has the pleasant perfume of a lotus. Not as disparaging as his descriptions of the men, I thought. But then Swami discussed the Elephant woman.

This category had a yoni of about twenty four centimetres in depth, large breasts, a broad face and short limbs; she is gluttonous, eats noisily and has a harsh and hard voice; she is not easily satisfied and has secretions that smells like, "elephants in a rut." Twenty five pairs of female eyes stared at him in stony silence.

Sceptical about the accuracy of these broad categorisations, yonis and linghams ordered by size and smell, it became apparent that size was not the major issue, after all. It was about a good match, which was: Hare and Deer; Bull and Mare; and Stallion and Elephant. You could mate a Deer with a Bull, but never a Deer with a Stallion. The good news was that there were sexual positions which enhance penetration and tantric exercises to compensate for the size of the lingham (if it is indeed too small). Similarly there are positions which enable more comfortable intercourse if the man is too big.

 In Brief: Teaching sessions at Tantra School were a delightful mixture of enlightenment, they were funny, could be embarrassing, but were also heart opening and warm. It was refreshing to be in a room full of people who simply show up to be honest and truthful about those aspects of themselves that caused shame. It was humbling to witness individuals when they suddenly encountered a truth, a moment which is encapsulated by, "Aha!"

The morning session over, it was "this man at lunchtime", with the sheets unchanged. I steeled myself. Lack of cleanliness was not to get in the way of Godliness. Swami announced an absence of blocks and deep wounding, there was nothing preventing me from feeling full body orgasms. Thus pronounced fit, piqued that I did not need to heal anything, Swami and I continued with our work.

During teaching sessions in the hall, I sometimes blushed when our eyes connected, but he remained completely neutral. I was aware that this man was a tantric partner only, and hoped that I would not be foolish enough to develop notions of romantic love.

The teachings covered many topics including energy bodies, tantric rules and rituals, formulas for male and female sexual vitality, yoga *asanas* for tantra, the effects of tantra on the physical and spiritual bodies and mantras for awareness, control and channelling. It was a lot to assimilate in a short space of time, but I felt up for the challenge.

Assuming his position on the throne, Swami opened one session with yet another corker. "The vagina, in tantra, cannot be flabby." I wonder if my vagina is flabby? I looked down, wincing at the ghastly word 'flabby'. Swami explained that the internal vagina has many muscles, that woman who do not train these muscles have a "flabby vagina". He regaled us with a story of certain ladies in Bangkok who performed with ping pong balls. They would insert five numbered ping pong balls into their yoni's in consecutive order, ball 5 being the last to go in. With their powerful vaginal muscles they would reverse the order, expelling first ball 1, then 2, 3, 4 and lastly ball 5. I had no desire to be a ping-pong girl, but I wondered how they developed these super-vaginas.

I did not have to wonder long. Swami belted out, "Yoni eggs and their corresponding exercises are an ancient Chinese practice, used by the Queen and her concubines, to STRENGTHEN THE VAGINA!" The practice remained a secret in the Royal Palace, its purpose being not only to please the King, but to strengthen the *Chi* muscle which lifts sexual energy inward and upward for its transmutation into higher spiritual energy." I toyed with the unlikely picture of Queen Elizabeth, Princess Anne and the Duchess of Cornwall discussing yoni egg exercises over high tea at Claridges. Shelving images of the royal elite, I resolved to purchase a yoni egg.

 In Brief: Our text books illustrated the practice very nicely. A thread would be passed through a hole running down the middle of the egg, and a weight attached to the end. Water bottles were suggested, as their weight could be easily adjusted. Egg inserted, the practitioner would stand, naked, in a horse-like stance and try to swing the weight north to south, then east to west, using the vaginal muscles. I thought I would look ridiculous.

I chose a lovely, solid jade egg, without a hole. The ritual of insertion proved to be a gentle process, taking about an hour. I could barely feel it, so attended yoga class with my egg. "What if I have an orgasm?" I asked my yoga instructor laughingly.

"If you do, enjoy it!"

 In Brief: The egg sits among my other crystals, now. Some pick up the jade egg, marvelling at its magnetism. I smile, its journey my secret.

During this intense week, I felt that I was on a sacred journey to the heart of that which made me a woman. I wished that every woman could make such a journey. Swami and I became regular lovers, enjoying a session a day if I was up to it. The week flew by, seeming to end barely before it had begun. The teaching had whet my appetite for yoga, for evolution itself and for the many mystic and ancient traditions. So I signed up for a one month yoga intensive, the first of 52 levels.

I had a feeling that I would be around for a while which meant that I needed a more permanent home. I visualised the perfect bungalow for my stay. It would be high up on a hill, with flowing white curtains and a bathroom made of stone. Puk (pronounced Pook) called to arrange a viewing of a home near the school. I followed her directions and headed up one of the few mountains in the area, riding up and up to reach the bungalow at the top. I made it up the steep driveway, parked and walked up a flight of beautiful teak stairs on the side of the house. The view from the deck took my breath away. Blue ocean stretched as far as the eye could see, dotted with distant islands, to my left and right were hills covered with palm trees. The deck itself was solid, well oiled, with a brilliant turquoise hammock swinging gently in one corner. Delighted, I climbed into the folds of the hammock, discovering that I could reach the teak beam that it was attached to. Rocking my cradle with my foot, I swung happily with my eyes closed. "You want look house?" The voice belonged to an elderly gentleman, Puk's father, peering down at me. "Yes!" I said, "I very much want look house," and I smiled and he smiled back.

He opened the glass doors to heaven. The dark teak walls and floors were a fitting backdrop for the white cotton curtains and teak four-poster bed draped in a white mosquito net. It was the perfect tantric lair. I inspected the curtains, uncharacteristic of Thai décor which favoured peach, green or blue chintz, admiring the detail, the light blue embroidered border, noting that all of the curtains matched. There were windows on all sides, with almost wall to floor windows facing the deck and affording a view of the gulf from inside the bungalow. The kitchen was standard, with a fridge and a wok. The bathroom had the appearance of being clad in stone, with the biggest showerhead I had ever seen and a beautiful, enormous mirror. I was used to little mirrors stuck onto cheap plastic bathroom cabinets, but I could see most of me in this one. Looking good, I thought.

This was going to be my new home. But I there was one more thing to check: the sheets. They were beautifully patterned, a baby blue filigree on a white background. As I looked at them, they quickly grew on me. Then I touched them. They were polycotton. Never mind, I would bring my white percale sheets from Samui. The deal was done.

19

Cult Mania

"Doll, dolly, doll doll doll, dolly doll!" Jo and I shrieked in delight, heading for her gold jeep, a wake of Peaceful Warrior essential oil spray behind us. Cackling loudly, with dancing hands, we sped off in the Golden Chariot, attracting the bemused attention of a few other drivers. I was on the island of Samui for a short while to catch up with friends (specifically Jo, Mark, Annabel and Elicia) and collect my belongings, Jo reliably collecting me from the local Samui port.

Jo was tall, slim, with long legs and a mane of curly dark hair, a British woman who had moved to Samui to work at the Spa. I had disliked her on sight and was not prepared to change my mind when I was first introduced to her over lunch. At JP's invitation, Joe arrived wearing flowing white trousers, a white top and a beautiful silk green shawl. She also wore a diamond nose stud and bindi. During lunch I had watched her closely, the way she seemed to delight in every mouthful, her long fingers gently wiping her mouth with her napkin, gazing at JP with her tiger eyes. Despite my initial reservations, from that lunch we became firm friends, spending time on the beach, swimming, eating, or lounging around her large bungalow, playing with her adorable cats, Tiger Jackson and CC Jasper Wild.

We headed straight for Art Café, which served the best raw food burritos and freshly squeezed juice. I regaled her with tales of Tantra School and Swami, size and technique, punctuated by Jo nodding, giggling and questioning.

I had to fit in a porch session with Brother Mark, drinking coconut and green smoothies, engaging in discussion that left me thoughtful, mindful. Mark and I worked on understanding and mastering the Law of Attraction; spoke of the human condition, the meaning of greatness; how to programme the mind; and the power of words. It was wonderful to spend time amongst my soul family!

My friend, Annabel, was from Britain, escaping a mad world. With an amazing amount of courage, she carved a career for herself on the island, singing and offering reiki. She was talented, with the sexiest jazz singing voice in the world, and I was grateful to count her as my friend. Meeting at a local hotel with a long marina stretching out into the sea, we soaked up the sun in our comfortable bean bags, apparently floating on the ocean. Here we had serious conversations about bikinis, boys, love and where to buy our next Goddess dress. Talking was interspersed with long, comfortable and dreamy silence, content with each other's company.

My friend Elicia was an American woman of Amazonian build. Her skin glowed, her legs reached my waist and when we hugged my face nestled between her large, firm breasts. She was an expert on detoxification, and I would swap coaching sessions for her advice. For my stay we had use of a luxurious villa (belonging to her current boyfriend). Built on a secluded plot, high up in the hills, on the northern side of the island, enormous black bells had been placed in every space. Time at The Bell House with Elicia meant lazing about, naked, on luxuriously thick day beds beside an infinity pool flamboyantly merging with the Gulf of Thailand. It was heaven, nowhere to be and nothing to do but enjoy the sunshine.

Elicia and I would also meet at our favourite quirky coffee shop in Lamai called Perk and Peck (the name gave no indication that it had anything to do with coffee). Occupying what was, I assumed, the downstairs lounge area of an apartment, it was furnished with bright peach leather sofas with cats everywhere. There were cats on the counter, on the floor, on the sofas and on the stairs. We went there primarily as it served soya milk and would save us the twenty minute drive to Starbucks in Chaweng. The owner was a gay Thai man and the shop, despite having an open sign on the door, seemed never to be open. On more than one occasion I could be seen repeatedly banging on the door in the early afternoon until Mr Perk or Mr Peck would sleepily open the door and make me a soya mocha. Elicia and I would stroke any cat which was tame, one of our favourites had his back left leg amputated in what was probably a motorbike hit and run. We would sit outside on the cool concrete garden furniture in an attempt to escape the faux leather and watch the hustle and bustle on the noisy street several meters away.

The two week interlude sped to its end, the days filled with fun and friendship. Throwing belongings haphazardly into the old black samsonite, I missed Mummy June's superlative packing skills. Bidding an energetic, noisy and tearful farewell to Jo (who had driven me to the local port), I boarded the ferry for the trip to my new home, yoga intensive, and Swami. From the upper deck I could see the next island, and I was precisely where I needed to be, doing exactly what I needed to do. I dropped into being present, beautifully calm, completely silent and deeply in the moment.

Arriving by taxi at my new home, the view astounding, the planet seemed infinite and radiantly remarkable. Later, housework and unpacking completed, I relaxed a while in the swinging hammock, before the meditation at the Shiva Hall.

It was a Full Moon Yang Spiral Meditation, Angel Gabriel informed me, hosted by the school. In white, as instructed, I followed the candle lit path to the hall. At night, filled with soft candle light, with net walls and thatched roof, the atmosphere was magical. Suddenly my delight and curiosity became tinged with reservation. I did not know what a cult was, but I remembered, from my childhood, that people floating about in white, performing candle-lit rituals, were sure to be engaging in black magic (at least). Perhaps I should proceed with caution. But I did not know what that meant either.

I found myself chatting easily to a woman in the line of Gemini people. I wondered why we had been separated according to our star signs, and she explained that the school had strong ties to yogic astrology. For this particular meditation we were divided into groups according to our predominant element.

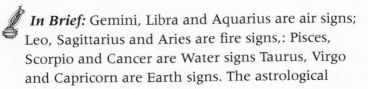 ***In Brief:*** Gemini, Libra and Aquarius are air signs; Leo, Sagittarius and Aries are fire signs,: Pisces, Scorpio and Cancer are Water signs Taurus, Virgo and Capricorn are Earth signs. The astrological

calendar starts with Aries (a fire sign) the next
month being earth then air and water.

Full moon parties were held on the south side of the island,
she told me. There the people would party hard, take drugs
and the energy they generated was chaotic, with people
dying, on occasion, from overdoses. We were balancing
out the energy generated on that side of the island, besides
contributing the additional power of group meditation into
the atmosphere. I nodded, understanding how the energy
a group generated could counteract chaos, and satisfied
that no one was going to be sacrificed.

The room became silent but electric. I composed myself
in a suitably impressive yoga pose, eyes closed, back of
hands on knees, index finger and thumb joined. But no
one paid the slightest bit of attention to me as I sat recit-
ing *Ooohhmm!* at the back of the Gemini line. Everyone
stood, the energy shifting into an excited and expectant
buzz as the Swami entered, wearing white. I almost leapt
up, waving, wanting the world to know that he was my
lover, but I thought better of it. He stood in the middle of
the room, the pinnacle, the participants beginning to move
around him, one elemental sign after the other, holding
hands, until we formed a spiral.

 In Brief: The spiral (I knew this from my Balinese
days of watching DVD's on sacred geometry with
Dodo) was an ancient structure that the universe
manifests on every level, from that of a molecule to
that of galaxies.

Hypnotic music filled the hall, I went still, clutching the
hands of the beings on either side of me. I could feel the

energy, a flow of yang rising up into my yin being. The rush of energy made me dizzy, I felt faint and dropped to my knees. With a huge effort I remained conscious, collapsing at the end of the hour-long meditation. Angel Gabriel was there when I opened my eyes, offering to drive me home. I felt simultaneously energized and utterly exhausted, grateful to be taken safely back to the bungalow.

The next morning I was up and ready, text book in hand, for the Yoga Intensive: six days a week; two hours in the morning; two hours in the afternoon; and a talk every night for one to two hours. Each day would begin with warm up exercises before a new asana, or position, was introduced. We would start with a simple asana, the *Padahastasana* (standing forward bend) and by the end of the month we would be doing *Sirsasana* (the head stand). I made a note of headstand dates with a "memo to self: wear a heavy-duty sports bra".

After introductions and a polite discussion of the curriculum, we went to a small hall, tucked away behind the yoga café, that was the venue for the course. The room had a concrete floor, netting in place of walls, a bathroom at the back, and a beautiful man adorning it. In white, fisherman pants, torso bare, blonde flowing hair and beard, he sat in a meditative pose, taking my breath away. I barely noticed the smell of the well used yoga mat that I placed close to the front. I did not want to miss a thing. He sat in silence with his eyes closed until the room settled. When he opened his stunningly beautiful blue eyes and spoke, I thought I would melt into that state of pure love Swami spoke of as *Samadhi*. He introduced himself as Jason and that is all I remember, my eyes stuck on his rippling muscles, my mind numb. I knew that he had stopped speaking when he stood, beginning the warm up practise. It was performed slowly, meditatively, a repetitive sequence with our eyes closed so the brain had nothing visual to latch onto and process. When Jason was giving the class I understood perfectly why the closed eyes policy was necessary. As we drew energy from the earth and the cosmos, I felt the flow through my energy centres. Closing with a meditation, I left the class floating on a cushion of bliss.

I still did not know what a cult was, and this bothered me. So I looked it up. Or rather, I checked a few sources. The first meaning that I found defined a cult as "a particular system of religious worship, especially with reference to its rites and ceremonies". So with that definition any religion could be called a cult, with rites and ceremonies such as the Christian baptism, a Jewish bar mitzvah, the Hindi death ritual and the Islamic marriage ritual. A cult was also classified as "a group or sect bound together by venera- tion of the same thing, person, ideal, etc." So followers of Star Trek would also be classified as cult members. A cult is also "a group having a sacred ideology and a set of rites centring around their sacred symbols". Does this include all religion and tradition? My research left me free to embrace any religion or sect I liked, including yoga, extracting that which fed my soul. I would leave the scaremongering and fear-based thinking behind me.

After a few days, I began to feel exhausted by the pro- gramme. Learning new *asanas* daily, attending lectures at night, I eagerly embraced all aspects of this ancient approach to life, but the schedule was intense. In spite of ten hours sleep a night, I needed to relax during the lunch break, heading for the local beach of Had Salad. Pulling up at "Salad" Beach, I walked up the white sands of the beach, sea meeting sky in the distance, the smell of clear water and baked sand nourishing my soul. Stepping through a clear stream as I approached the restaurant (this one had proper flush toilets, a big plus), I headed for my favourite table. It was hot, but cooler air flowed through the restaurant, which had no walls, and I sat facing the beach.

Ordering water and lime juice, and a vegetable stir fry with brown rice, my mind was struggling with the concept of dualism. I heard it spoken of in the evening lectures, but could not grasp its meaning. As if in answer to my need for illumination, I remembered a book that I carried in my bag. Dusting beach sand off it, I opened it to read: "Out beyond right and wrong is a field, I will meet you there." The book was *Rumi: The Book of Love*. The words penetrated me, swirling around my insides. I believed in right and wrong. Right was my target weight, not swearing (a lot), world peace, winning money, being healthy, paying all bills on time, angels, wearing matching bra and knickers, and drinking green juice. Wrong was getting sick, being late for things, the bird flu, demons, having an accident, having an accident whilst driving someone else's car and talking with my mouth full. By dividing everything into either right or wrong, I realised that I created a rollercoaster ride in which I could not accept a situation without judgement.

 In Brief: By taking away a label of *right* or *wrong* in any given situation I had embraced *is-ness*. *Is-ness* meant accepting the unfolding, having deep trust in the process of life, getting off the roller coaster ride of good or bad events. This new belief system still allowed me to feel pain, but removed the very destructive force of internal suffering.

Insight: This level of consciousness allowed me internal freedom and a life without fear. It allowed for non-attachment, it allowed me to move through life with utter trust. Crucially, embodying this principal gave me peace and made me whole.

After lunch I rode back to my beautiful bungalow, resting a while in the hammock, connecting with sky and angels, at ease. It felt as though I had barely laid down before I needed to rise again and set off for the afternoon class.

Sun low in the sky, a lovely, soft and warm teacher led us through a sun salutation – with a twist. Facing East, we were to chant the twelve Vedic names of the sun in each posture. It was an honouring of the Sky God that kept us warm, grew our crops and unfailingly rose each morning. I liked the idea of paying homage to the sun, listening carefully as our angel teacher explained the sequence. Every chant started with *"Aum"* and ended in *"Namah"*, in-between which we cleverly slotted one of the twelve names, simultaneously holding the particular position. Angel teacher told us not to worry as she would give us the Vedic name just before each chant. So we began, hands in prayer position and she gently said *"Mitraya"*. We followed with, *"Aum Mitraya Namah."* This first round of chanting was muddled, with everyone going at a different pace. By the time we reached, *"Haranyagabhaya"* it got plain messy. But we mumbled through and were pleased enough with ourselves when we were done after two hours.

In Brief: Sometimes this practice drew an intense psychic connection to the sun, with the background of voices penetrating my soul.

Swami was in Europe, visiting his parents, which was a good thing since our schedule was so full that I would have been hard-pressed to fit him in (pardon the pun).

Sitting with friends at the Yoga Café one Saturday evening, we saw the large figure of Swami. As he got closer, we realised that in spite of being of similar size, with the same gait and appearance, this was a much younger version than our Swami. Was this his love child? No, said one of the teachers, it was his nephew. He was the spitting image of Swami.

Nephew joined in classes, noisy, big, his energy over-powering. He had neither the ability to do yoga nor tact. Teachers had to bite their tongues while the obnoxious Nephew shared his knowledge, attempting to take over the teaching of theory, quickly earning the nickname, Teenage Mutant Ninja Swami.

We could tell when Teenage Mutant Ninja Swami was at the expensive bungalow that Swami had rented for him by the fresh pile of used pizza boxes piled up on the porch. The students never ate pizzas, so when a pizza delivery man was spotted in the neighbourhood we could be certain of the direction he was taking. I wondered about his prowess with ladies, and if his uncle had schooled him in the ancient arts of tantra, since it was clear that he had not got the hang of yoga.

The coordinator of our Shakti meeting, a sacred woman's circle, gathered us around during a meeting. She had a confidential question to ask, she said, that must, on no account, leave the room. We were curious. "I need a volunteer," she said, "There is a young man who needs to be deflowered." I gulped, it must be Teenage Mutant Ninja Swami. This was going to be a hard sell! The person who agreed to perform this ritual would be taught under the personal tutelage of the Swami, she promised. We waited for the offer of a large cash compensation. None was made, no hands were raised. Sounding desperate, she ran through a list of pro's – a very short list – and I wondered if, in the absence of a volunteer, the performance of this vital ritual would fall squarely on her shoulders. Or should I say, delicate cough, right between her legs. No one took the bait, she would be left to deliver the news.

Now we knew the reason for the presence of Teenage Mutant Ninja Swami. If he was ceremoniously deflowered, it was kept very, very, quiet. He came and went from classes, ate a lot of pizza, ignoring the school's dietary advice completely, then leaving several weeks later.

As the weeks passed by, I became lighter, leaving my dark life, the dark ages and darkness in general behind me. I became allergic to black, the colour feeling murky, perhaps because of the predominantly black wardrobe that I had possessed in my old city life. Now my face glowed. Moving from the dark to the light was a dangerous time, as both Anna and Dr A had warned me. I was to discover that bike accidents, bizarre kinetic movement of objects and being called in the night by the intangible, merely hinted at what was still to come.

20

The Soul Snatcher

I woke suddenly; it was the middle of the night and the shadows outside impenetrable. I was terrified, my body instantly and nauseatingly aware of danger. I sensed I was not alone and my gaze instinctively shot towards the glassed front door. On the other side of the glass, I saw an insect-like figure that radiated the darkness of ages, a blackness deeper than the night, black that consumed all light. Painfully thin, the spiky creature moved stealthily, emanating a malignant strength as it pushed a chair against the glass doors of the bungalow. Blood drained from my body, pooling in my heart and stomach. Breaking into a fearful sweat I watched the demonic apparition reach upwards to the latch on the double doors.

I closed my eyes and he was there. When I opened them he was there. Rivers of icy dread ran off my skin, an outpouring of dark energy that nourished the demon at the door. In seconds it would enter and claim my soul, dragging me back to that unspeakably vile dimension that I had narrowly escaped from. "Love is my protection," I whispered weakly. It did not falter, was about to enter the room. Screaming then, with all of the conviction I could muster, "I AM THE LIGHT, I SERVE THE LIGHT, I LOVE THE LIGHT, I LOVE MYSELF, I LOVE GOD, I AM ONE WITH GOD!"

In answer to my fervent prayer, an angel exploded into the room. In an instant her fiercely protective light dissolved the dread in my bones. The demon had been banished. Rigid, unable to move, I watched her place a large red candle on the dresser. The wick burst into flame, its radiance spreading through the room into the night, escaping through the cracks of the bungalow. Turning to me, I felt a godlike presence engulfing my heart. You need love. I felt three hard taps on my forehead sending waves of ecstatic bliss through my being. This was pure unconditional love. I slept, held in the arms of the mother.

I woke the next morning, instinctively rubbing my forehead. It felt a little tender. I got out of bed and moved to my front door, finding a heavy, wooden chair rammed up against the glass. With a thudding heart I tried to open the door, but it was locked from the outside. Trembling, I climbed through the window onto the deck, dragging the deck-chair several metres to its place at the outside table. Unlocking the door I let the air swirl through the previous night's battle ground. Nothing to do now except shower, dress, drink some urine, eat rice and attend my next yoga class. Chop wood, carry water.

Swami was back, sending a loving request for me to meet him at his bungalow at 15:00, which had become my usual slot. I complied with a sense of moving through my time with this powerful man that my Ego had called in. Our love making was meditative, almost divine, but I had not yet experienced that earth shattering moment that

I waited for. Nor had he massaged the hard knots in my yoni, declaring joyously that I had no blocks to remove.

He greeted me wearing an orange head band, a ridiculous shirt bearing a cartoon Krishna and, shockingly, nothing else, his lingham gaily swaying in the breeze. Since we were not having a relationship, I was unable to ask him if he was offering homage or disrespect. As I entered the bedroom I saw a figure slipping out of the study. Oh, how very awkward this was, I thought, hiding behind the chintz bedroom curtains, while the student departed.

The clean sheets surprised me. This was better than fighting demons and more pleasurable than yoga class, so I allowed myself to dissolve into the moment. We made love, he expertly entering me, arousing me, feeding me energy. I experienced huge vibrations in the entire region of my pelvis, the energy beginning to rise and fall. This was, he said, the start of the mind-blowing stuff which he experienced. I had begun to harbour the sneaky suspicion that my body would not allow me to feel this earth shattered phenomena with this particular man.

I continued attending classes during this exploration with Swami. We were taught kriyas, or cleanses, during the course of the yoga intensive, beginning with scraping the tongue each morning. This kriya would be followed by cleansing of nostrils using the Neti Pot, then Vamana Dhauti. Halfway through the course, we were introduced to a powerful new kriya, Amaroli, by Jason The Tantra God. The class looked glum as Jason instructed us to drink a cup of our own urine on waking. The procedure was to collect the urine midstream, as it were, not at the beginning of urination.

In Brief: The Neti Pot was used to pour a mixture
of warm water and salt into one nostril, allowing it
to drain from the other. The *Vahum Daute* required
quickly swallowing a litre and a half of water and
then vomiting it back up. Having been bulimic at
one stage in my past, the reflex came naturally
for me. *Amaroli* (Urine therapy) is well known as
a cure for many aliments. While convinced of the
benefits, I had never brought myself to practice it.

Closing the morning session, Jason asked us to put any
suggestions in the box. He would see us for a report back
on Urine Therapy 101 the next day. I thought better of
requesting that the big man wore pants when receiving
female guests, distracted by the laughter of a small group
around a fellow student. His suggestion was read aloud,
"Please could Jason wear a shirt to class and give the rest of
the guys a chance with the girls."

I purchased a special cup for my new morning drink.
I drank extra water that night, in spite of consisting on a
plain diet of brown rice, soya sauce, fruit and vegetables.
Rising at 07:00, I scraped my tongue, douched my nose,
vomited my water and then made a wee. Halfway through
I collected a good cupful, setting the cup on the bathroom
table. I stared into the mirror, wondering what on earth I
was doing. I unscrewed my herbal toothpaste tube, then
balked at drinking the morning champagne. I left the bathroom, deciding I could not go through with this and began
preparing a breakfast of oats, staring out at the gulf of
Thailand. Suddenly I put the bowl down, marched into the
bathroom, picked up the cup and downed it. It tasted like
urine and it was warm. Heaving, I gulped some toothpaste.

I was going to do whatever it took for the evolution of my soul! I was not to be put off by a little wee!

Only half the students had tried it on that first day, but I continued the practice, experiencing a deeper connection with my body. One night I consumed a large slice of pizza and an ice cold beer (my first and last at yoga school) The next morning my urine smelt terrible and tasted foul. The cooked cheese, wheat and alcohol had a distinct effect on my system, reflected by markedly higher levels of salt in my urine, which was also bitter from the alcohol.

The next challenge was to follow a specific diet, the Oswara Diet number 7, an eating regimen that ostensibly cured cancer. Keen to hear the intricacies of this extraordinary diet, I was surprised at the short explanation. A very short explanation, consisting of only two words: brown rice. That was it, we were to eat brown rice for the last ten days of the course. We were, however, allowed two seasonings, soya sauce and sesame seeds, the class rushing to purchase the suddenly desirable ingredients. This was a simple diet plan: brown rice for breakfast, lunch and supper. No points to count, no calories, no funny little lunch bars. Just rice. This had a remarkable effect on me, I felt centred, grounded, solid, present and open.

After one month of boot camp for yoginis, I graduated along with my peers. The hall alight with thousands of candles, adorned with swathes of white material, the Swami personally presented each graduate with a certificate, and gift of a school shirt and bag.

I did not want the journey to end, enrolling for the next level and extending my lease. I was in it for the long haul.

21

The Bloody Period

The next level was a deeper exploration of the ancient practice of white spiritual tantra as well as exploration into the mind, meditation, and consciousness. It seemed yogi's were conscious while they ate, had sex and when they slept and crucially when they died. A far cry from the manic Western existence of only past and future. I was also increasingly able to sense and move energy, my physic awareness growing.

Many of the exercises required pairing up with another. During one of these, I closed my eyes, suddenly seeing an image of a cracked pelvis floating before me. This skeletal form flashed at me three times, followed by a pair of small, sickly lungs, also appearing in space three times. These visuals were unaccompanied by voices, commentary or speech bubbles, in short there was nothing to guide me as to what they were about. So, when it came time to share our experiences, I told my partner what I had seen. She lifted her top, revealing horrific scars, the result of a broken pelvis; she had also had surgery on her lungs, she said, showing those scars as well. Crikey! What to do?

The morning following that experience, I found that I could see the energy bodies of my classmates. They were about an inch thick, a luminous greeny-grey sheen. This urine therapy sure is powerful, I thought. The energy bodies bulged in places, had indentations in others. Some people moved faster than their energy body, which would follow their movements slowly, sometimes taking time to catch up with them. Some energy bodies moved in perfect timing with the body. I would have visions during the day, some indecipherable, some with a clear message. Sometimes these visions would happen when I touched people and sometimes when I was riding my bike. I was clairvoyant and clairaudient. Maybe I should change my name to Claire. I felt like a super power, toying with the idea of wearing my underpants on the outside, like Superwoman.

Insight: I realised that everyone is multisensory. I was beginning to experience my natural state. I understood how an unhealthy lifestyle constricts energy flow.

Menstruation as a Pathology. At this introduction, most of the women in the class bristled. We had been taught that copious bleeding accompanied by pain was normal menstruation. Not according to the ancient texts, however, which claimed that a small amount of blood is normal as we could transmute the menstrual love back into the body and use it for energy. Swami asked us to note how we felt during menstruation. Tired, sore, grumpy and at the mercy of "the curse", was the answer. "The process of menstruation," said Swami, "is the loss of perfectly good blood and the perpetual cause of distress." I had to agree. He spoke

passionately on the deleterious effects of diet and civilisa-
tion on menstruation. The lecture was long, emphasising
the theory that we need not have to bleed for five days to
be healthy. A couple of drops would be totally normal.

The group split, the men leaving the room to discuss
"man stuff". A senior female teacher, who was also a
medical doctor, continued on the topic of menstruation.
"This blood, as well as semen, is seen as vital life force
energy," she opened with, "it is potent liquid energy." Then
she dropped the bombshell: "Tantrikas and their partners
drink menstrual blood to conserve their vitality. This is a
practice we encourage in this school."

There was a shocked silence. This was an archaic practice,
surely, disgusting, unnatural and bizarre. Sheer Madness.
There was no way I could partake in this revolting practice.

Breaking the incredulous silence, the teacher, glowing
with health and vitality, asked if there were any observa-
tions. One of the younger woman in the group raised her
hand. She had dreadlocks, large tattoos – the archetypical
earth child – saying that she had lived with a tribe in South
America for a couple of months. She used a mooncup, and
went into the forest to empty her cup during her menstruation. When she gave the blood back to the earth, pouring
the contents onto the ground, the women of the tribe went
mad, laughing, screeching and pointing at her and the
ground. They did not speak English, so she could not tell
what was happening. A couple of hours later, she needed
to empty the cup again, setting off into the forest, followed
closely by a group of women. Before she could discard the
blood, a woman took the mooncup from her, and shared the
contents with the other women. She was shocked, but on
her return, consulting an holistic gynaecologist, she found

that this practice had been normal, that it was not unhealthy, and that some encouraged it. She had been drinking her blood ever since.

We gawped at her. I could see the logic, could even respect the ritual, but I would not partake of it.

Still shaken from the day's teachings, waiting in the queue at the yoga school shop to pay for my sesame seeds, I spotted the moon cups. I bought one, not knowing why. Dr A would be proud, perhaps considering me well on the path to becoming an evolved woman: a couple of drops of blood; no tampons; and all that.

Later, scrubbing my body under the gloriously large shower head, I noticed menstrual blood running down my leg. The teachings of the day rang in my head as I watched my energy, the liquid that could magically nourish an embryo, spill onto the tiled floor and out through the drain. This essence did not belong in a sewer. I began using the mooncup that full moon night.

Before bed I spent minutes in the head stand pose. It helped remove anxiety.

The next morning I experienced heightened perception, aware of my surroundings with all of my senses. Completing the daily cleansing regimen, I removed the mooncup, studying the warm, bright red blood. It smelt musty with the distinct odour of iron. Standing at the mirror, I looked myself squarely in the eyes, dedicating this primal essence to the Goddess. I held the cup to my lips, tipped it back and swallowed.

I felt a little weird, swallowed some mineral water and brushed my teeth. I felt proud of myself, a powerful Goddess indeed.

The topics for the day were love and possession, jealousy and open relationships, contentious issues which sparked emotional and heated debate. "What does the word 'jealousy' mean for you," asked Swami. Eyes closed, feeling into the word, I was satisfied that I was not a jealous person. But the story of Jean, a friend of Mummy June, rose in my mind.

Mummy June said it was a big deal for Jean to stay over. Jean arrived for dinner, beautiful, vital, and nervously commenting that her husband Frank was uncomfortable with the arrangements. His discomfort became apparent when she ignored the first three calls on her mobile with trepidation, finally answering the fourth time, then leaving the phone upstairs. By the time the home phone rang, a mere half hour later, our little coven of three was in full swing, wine and music flowing. When I told Jean's husband that he could not speak to her as we were busy, he responded with a torrid stream of abuse and the accusation that she was with another man. What an asshole, I thought, shocked. He called constantly during the evening, wanting assurance from my mother that there were no men there. Early the next morning Frank called to say he had fallen, but was not hurt, please could she come home. She left hastily after breakfast.

Mum told me that Jean was fifteen when she met Frank, twenty when they married. Frank had forbidden Jean to have a male doctor or male hairdresser. He called her constantly when she was out of the home, accompanied her everywhere, discouraging female gatherings where he could not attend for fear that a secret

lover would be present. He also held the purse strings
and Jean had never worked. She had to "perform"
regularly even though Frank had to take a pill in order
to have sex. She was 70.

Swami interrupted the class debate on jealousy and possession. "You have no idea about what love is, love does not
know possession, love does not know jealously. Love is not
something that comes to you. Love is always there, only
YOU block it. Western society has serialised and glamorised
love. Your Barbie and Ken childhoods have programmed
you to believe that love is something that it is not. Romanticism has become the religion of the West, it has left a
confused generation in its wake." Sweating (as always), he
continued his diatribe, "You know nothing of love because
you know NOTHING of yourselves, always clinging to a
pathetic hope that you will feel Oneness through another.
I will speak the words of Osho," holding up a book, reading
loudly, "LOVE IS NOT A RELATIONSHIP, it is a state of
being. When you fall in love with a woman, you fall in love
with everything, with all women. This woman is a symbol
of all women. And she is a human being, SO YOU FALL
IN LOVE WITH ALL HUMAN BEINGS. Your love energy
is released to all. THIS IS TRUE LOVE." He was on a roll,
"Possessive love is NOT true love, it is so tiny, it suffocates
itself and it suffocates the other. You are NOT another's
possessions."

Swami did the hair flick and took a gulp of water, "You
have been taught possessive love by your parents. They
have said, 'Love me I am your mother,' or 'Who do you
love more, your mother or your father?' These are the
wrrrrrrong questions to ask a child. The quantification of

love is WRONG. Everybody is possessive, they say, 'Love me and no one else.' This thinking is connected to a NEU-ROTIC relationship. Anyone connected to an exclusive relationship is IMMATURE. We think this is dangerous because it goes against our habits. WHO CREATED THESE HABITS? Anyone who lives this way is in a state of scarcity and LACK."

At the outset I had been warned that Tantra would confront me with fundamental questions about my life, about man, and about the Universe. I was struggling with my relationship with Swami, knowing he had other lovers. By the time Swami stopped talking, I was crying, vulnerable, confused, with everything that I thought I knew about love and relationships turned on its head.

After the break I sat quietly amongst my group of women, too bruised to speak. A slightly older woman began to talk. She was young when she married her ex-husband. They were Christians, and she knew nothing of sex before her wedding night. The church that they belonged to instructed that she obey her husband. He liked sex and he liked it often, once every day or every other day. She, however, had a different rhythm, but nonetheless give in to his demands without a fight for the sake of keeping him happy. He also liked to drink, frequently staggering in late at night, forcing her to have sex, reminding her that this was one of the duties of a wife.

"So you were raped through your entire marriage".

We bore silent witness as the woman's face slowly crumpled at the truth in these words, dissolving into suppressed feelings.

"Until recently it was not a crime to rape your wife," remarked one of the women. For many women in this world it is normal to be subjected to rape, the act supported by a patriarchal and religious structure because they had entered into a religious and lawful contract with a man.

An older woman led us in a ritual prayer. Joining hands, we repeated, "Please give us the strength to say these words, 'This is not OK for me'. By doing this for myself I give strength to men and women everywhere to do the same". I looked around the circle of women, this powerful circle of sisters, all eyes moist, in deep gratitude that I was free to choose my own experience.

That night seemed perfect for experiencing true love at Bhajans, a devotional singing ritual, held by a neighbouring yoga school. It was easy to find, joining the joyful stream of bikers in fisherman trousers, girls with bhindis and wild tresses. We parked in a forest, high on a mountain, and I spotted some friends. Laughing, we climbed the long path, well lit with magical fire, finally emerging before a white, pyramid shaped structure. Ducking through the narrow door of the cob structure, the energy palpable, the full force of voices raised in bliss struck. It was crowded, with yoginis sitting hip to hip, swaying and chanting in time with the music. Sacred symbols surrounded us, the dark night sky, brilliant with stars, visible through windows set high in the structure. My throat opened fully, chants poured out of me, a devotion to ourselves, to the divine, to our brothers and sisters. The very walls hummed, vibrating with us as we lost ourselves in music and boundless love. It was a magical, mystical and spiritual experience. I felt pure love.

22

In spite of the experience of deeply satisfying meditative states, I was increasingly disillusioned with my encounters with Swami. The decision to engage at all was driven by ego, the need of Titanic woman to conquer the Alpha male. But how could I break up a relationship that I was not having? So I simply told him that I could not continue with our sessions. Looked disappointed, he asked, "Why?"

"Because I can't feel your heart. It's closed, " I said, unpremeditated, the words springing out of nowhere.

"No one has ever said that to me," he said, wounded now.

"Well, I am telling you."

"Thanks for the feedback." Formal, dismissive.

I interpreted it as fuck off, leaving his bungalow with a sense of loss, a little tear of self pity running down my cheek. If I could not have an earth-moving-making-love-with-the-Gods experience with Swami, then I never would.

I was beginning to find the routine and grinding daily practice a little tedious. The school and it's community kept me busy. What little free time I had I spent reading, swinging in my hammock, exploring the island and just hanging out with a select group of friends and the odd lover.

Aurelia and her partner Patrick were a couple that seemed like the bedrock of our yogic community Aurelia was a champion raw food chief and one of the most beautiful women that I knew. I accepted an invitation for one of the usual pot luck dinners, knowing that I would find love and friendship. Arriving late, I was ushered to the only free space, right beside a man who I had seen at school, and whom I had taken an instant dislike to. Gigantic, well over six foot four, sporting a plaited beard and with features that seemed vaguely Native American, I could not believe that we would have anything in common.

Having no choice, I sat down. He smiled, introducing himself as Red. "Grace," I said, bowing slightly. Eating in silence, at first, the conversation picked up, and I discovered that Red was well educated, exceptionally bright, was a spiritual leader in his community and was involved in Exopolitics.

 In Brief: Exopolitics deals with the interplanetary confederation of beings who visit Earth. It is a science which should not be dismissed as the rantings of a bunch of crazy people. The internet has allowed consciousness from around the globe to connect on this very matter. I for one was listening. Dr A had also spoken to me of these things. More and more people are taking this seriously.

His tantric partner had suggested he spend time with the physical disciplines of breath, yoga and tantra. He listened to my stories about the time with Dr A, and seemed to understand the processes that I had undergone. When I spoke about the ritual with *Iboga*, he seemed impressed, and I liked that. "It's a karmic cleanser," he added, "I don't believe it's an hallucinogenic. Whatever you see is coming out of you." I shuddered. He spoke little of himself, I believe he was shy. We parted when the evening came to an end, but I hoped that I would see more of him. I had been very drawn to him, had enjoyed his company, despite my early reservations. I felt ashamed at the judgments I had formed based on his appearance.

I encountered him several times over the next few days and our friendship began to grow.

A couple of weeks after the dinner, I was startled awake by a loud thump on my balcony in the middle of the night. The room looked blurred, like the picture on a television screen, but I knew that I was not dreaming when I felt the teak floor beneath my bare feet. On my way to fetch a glass of water, I glanced over my shoulder towards the window. My heart leapt into my throat when I saw a figure standing on the deck. It was over 2 metres tall, blue, with a massive head, no discernible mouth, and it stared at me through enormous, slanted, almond-shaped eyes. I stared at "him" for what felt like hours, my heart rate calming, knowing he was a"friendly"

"Algernon Blackwood." The words were delivered telepathically.

What the fuck…? I thought better than asking him in for a cup of tea, and stayed where I was on the bed. Perhaps it was an introduction, perhaps it was his name. In my head, I formed my name, Grace G. Payge. Now we were both staring, he at me, me at him. I saw him, then I saw something else. He showed me the planet he came from, not dissimilar to earth. I found myself on the shore of a vast ocean of water-like liquid, a strange light that seemed to come from within the sand, the plants and the stars. There was no night and day, everything sparkled and the sand was whiter than any I had ever seen. The trees sparkled as well with that inner light. There was no hint of aggression in this place, there was no fighting, no wars, no famine and no lack. Two beings approached that looked like Algernon, around 7 foot tall, blue and slightly transparent. Sparkling, gliding with the fluidity of quicksilver, their sex was not discernible. Their heads were slightly triangular in shape, with only large, deep black and kind eyes in their faces. They did not speak to me but I felt an imprint in me, a feeling of "home" on this planet of the super conscious.

Abruptly I dropped back onto my bed, Holy shit! The alien at the glass window had disappeared. I felt as though I was in a trance as I reached for the book beside my bed. Page 84. I found page 84, my heart skipping a beat as I read, "Algernon Blackwood wrote of intelligent beings who pre-existed mankind on Earth, 'of such great powers or beings there may conceivably be a survival, of which poetry and legend alone caught a flying memory and called them Gods, Monsters, Mythical Beings of all sorts and kinds.'"

I was beside myself, certain that I was heading for another breakdown. It felt like I was trapped between two worlds, my home and Earth. Red answered my call, and I wailed, "I've been abducted by Algernon." I may have been screaming hysterically.

"Come over, now," he said. I flew out of the house in my pyjamas, leaving the doors open, leapt onto my bike and screamed down the hill. I ran straight into his arms, my body still heaving uncontrollably.

In an attempt to bring me back to earth, we walked on the beach. Red's strong body pressed up against me from behind, his huge arms enveloped me as we stood facing a wind-whipped ocean, frothy in the dark night. Lightening flashed across the night sky and simultaneously through me. We were breathing as one, the boundary between *me*, *him* and nature dissolving periodically. My body was pulsating with Universal energy. I was engulfed in nature's entirety as she moved in me and swirled around me. I began to calm down, and Red guided me to his beach hut.

"My little lightening conductor," he said. I smiled as we entered his earthy space, filled with candles and lamps. I lay on his bed, feeling the coarse beach sand between my toes, as he made tea. While I sipped my comforting brew he said, "I'll get the lights." Obeying my mental command the lights switched off. "I love how you do that" Red said. In the gentle candle light my eyes filled with tears, "I want to go home." His tangible empathy had me crying all the more.

"How can this be home, the paradoxical place we live in? Such beauty, such power and yet such anger, aggression, needless violence, sadness." Red invited me to lie down, curling around me and holding me in archangel strength. The smell of incense soothed my troubled mind into a dream world. For the first time I fell asleep in another's arms, but was unsure if Red was mortal.

I awoke the next morning still in his arms. Turning to him, I opened my eyes. I touched him, his face, his chest, his arms. He was really there, solid, present. An electric energy passed through my fingers, waking him. Eyes meeting, silently exchanging a deep sense of what was unfolding, we sat up, moving into yab yum, fully clothed. Time stopped. Instantly we flipped from solid reality and existed only for the moment.

It hit me hard. I was not merely living in the present.

I was presence.

Connected, we created a vortex of circulating energy, touching each other with spirit, touching each other's souls. Merging with the divine. I, Goddess, the divine feminine; he, God, the divine masculine. Hours and hours of ecstasy flowing into each other, a rapturous meeting with the Beloved in true, pure, orgasmic love. God heroin coursing through the electric fibre of my being. It felt like my heart was orgasming, incomparable to anything I had ever experienced.

Slowly, our energy bodies returning to us, I found Red at my feet, holding on, head bowed. "Thank you for showing me Shakti again," he said, tears of gratitude running down his face.

This was the kind of sex Swami had talked about, any nakedness or penetration would have seemed lewd, rude and utterly human. My heart had broken open.

I had experienced God first hand. In my polka dot pyjamas.

23

Two weeks after my friendly visit from Algernon, I busied myself preparing brown rice and soya for breakfast, but could not shake off a strong sense of foreboding. I had a certainty that something awful was happening, and that it could result in my death. It felt as though I was coming down with flu, so climbed back into bed, waking again around 14:00, surprised that I had slept so long. Reaching for my mobile phone I was startled by the sharp pain that shot through my arm and down my spine. With difficulty I moved slowly to the fridge for a bottle of water, exhausted by the time I got there. I drank, worried about dehydrating, and went back to sleep. The next day I lay in bed, moving slowly, feeling that my bones were slowly crumbling.

It took twenty minutes to get from my bungalow, down the stairs and onto my bike. Intent on getting to the chemist, I did not consider that operating a motor bike in my condition, driving it down one of the steepest hills on the island, may be dangerous. By the time I reached the shop I was in agony, could barely speak, but managed to ask for rehydration salts. I clutched the counter, feeling faint, my head between my knees in a strange crouching stance, the assistant at the chemist helplessly looking on. I succeeded in paying for my purchase, but failed on my first attempt to leave the shop, knocking over a stand of cheap sunglasses. I made it on the second attempt, stumbling out of the chemist, into the street. Then I passed out on the pavement.

Reluctantly I allowed myself to be driven to the one and only doctor on the island, where my blood was siphoned and a diagnosis of dengue fever was delivered. A stay in hospital was strongly recommended, "In case things should take a turn for the worst." I ignored the suggestion and went home to suffer.

Waking the next day in pain my hands and arms were covered with red bloody pin pricks. This was, I guessed, the "turn for the worse".

Staring my possible mortality squarely in the arm, I felt Death calling me from this life and into another. Muddled and confused, I wondered if I was dying. Accepting this I felt peaceful. My love for my mother was palpable, accompanied by a tangible feeling that I had done the very best I could with the life I had been given. I was soothed by this as the beautiful grip of death squeezed the life from my body, birthing me into the skies as a surge of concentric energy. Death: the ultimate, exquisite, transformer.

Hours later I returned to my body with the realisation that I needed to get to the hospital. Now. It was my single thought. Faced with death, I wanted life. Faced with life I wanted death. But I had seen that death was an illusion, there was only life. I wondered if the confusion was caused by the fever or was it a Gemini thing?

Finally accepting I needed medical attention, I called the Heavenly Torso. In a flash, the topless Jason arrived. As he helped me down the steps of the bungalow I heard a familiar, but unidentified, rustling in the scrub. A three foot, heavy set lizard appeared at the bottom of the stairs, his forked tongue dancing from his mouth. We stopped, watching the creature in silence.

"I see the witch has a dragon," Jason said. I smiled weakly at my dragon as he graciously made way for his ailing witch.

There was only one hospital and it stood in the middle of a coconut grove. It had an "emergency" section where I was poked and prodded and filled with strange fluids. Suitably drugged up I was moved to the single, basic, ward. No food was provided, there were no curtains for privacy, no drinks trolleys, no comfortable beds. A redeeming feature was flush toilets. I spotted what looked like private rooms outside, but was disappointed to find that they were full. I would have to suck it up in the cheap seats.

Pain free I soon became bored and, wheeling a drip, I moved outside to the open air corridor which resembled a festive picnic site. Families of patients were setting up home for the night with bamboo mats, steaming rice bowls, papaya, hot drinks strewn everywhere. I moved closer to the private rooms in the hopes that I would be able to wangle my way into one. There were eight pairs of shoes outside the first room, the music played at full volume and lights flashing through the drawn curtains. The second room was pretty much the same. The parties would continue late into the night. Maybe "private room" meant something entirely different in Thailand.

Feeling sorry for myself I nestled back into my bed, surrounded by fifteen other women and two newborn babies. When the pain level rose again, I approached the glassed-in nurses station. All three nurses were furiously typing on Facebook chat and looked visibly annoyed at my gentle knocking on the door. "What you want?" the first nurse shouted through a closed door. "I am in pain, feeling funny, like I am dying." No response from Matron Despot. Maybe a direct question would help, "Will I die?" She rolled her eyes, "Sometimes die, most time not die." She opened the door and shoved two painkillers in my hand.

I feel asleep in the early hours of the morning, slipping into the now familiar sensation of being sucked up into the atmosphere. I moved through thick layers of dense bliss, intensely pleasurable, surfing a high vibrational cosmic body fuck. I wanted to stay in this state until the end of time.

I regained consciousness at day break. Bummer. Still alive and living on Planet Shitsville with no peace, no bliss. I was certain that I would live, so I discharged myself. I texted Swami to tell him of the disease, secretly hoping for a gentle stroll, a light dinner, a mopped brow and a long bath. He responded that the only cure was orgasms. Many and often. He would be more than happy to assist me with this sexual healing route. I politely declined.

Back home I slept, feeling that I had learnt what I needed to and that my time in this place was over. The sudden need to leave surprised me, a little, but I did not aspire to complete all 52 levels at Tantra School. For some reason India called to me. But so with dengue fever, such a trip was inadvisable.

I wanted to see my mum, brother and father. I had not intended using my return ticket, but I checked that it was valid. I called my brother and told him what I wanted to do. I was to surprise Mummy June by strolling into the kitchen in four days time.

I was weak, but managed to pack, the bone pain had gone and I was hydrated. I said my goodbyes, with Jo picking me up in Samui, where I would spend one night. I met my friends for one last supper and flew to Bangkok early the next morning. From there I caught the 12-hour flight to London. I slept fitfully on the plane, still feeling ill, disorientated and shocked by my sudden urge to go home.

As we landed in Heathrow I felt sick, nervous in the awareness that I had changed dramatically. Now I was a size 10, tanned, with life-changing experiences behind me. I collected my bags from the carousel and wheeled my trolley through to the arrivals hall, spotting my good looking brother at a distance. He held a large bunch of beautiful flowers, eagerly looking out for me. He walked straight past me. "Don," I yelled. He swung around with a sharp intake of breath, "I didn't recognize you!" We hugged and chatted, I was grateful for the flowers.

He had told mum that he was taking her out for dinner that evening. I was nervous when we pulled up outside Mummy June's house, and he walked through the conservatory. From the kitchen I heard him say that he had a surprise for her.

I stepped through the kitchen door and Mummy June started screaming. As she launched herself at me, she screamed louder, "My darling, my darling, my darling, I felt you coming closer to me, I knew it was you!" When she had calmed down we went out to eat. I had bumped up the diet to vegetarian recently, otherwise I would have struggled with anything on the menu. We ate, held hands and Mum repeated over and over, "My darling!"

Mum insisted on making up the bed with fresh white sheets and I collapsed into bliss.

The next morning I was disorientated and dengue sore, a combination of headaches and a dull pain that seemed to come from the very bone. I was also easily exhausted, so in the 3 months that it took to recover, I watched a lot of day time TV. I was surprised to find that I had come back to a nation obsessed with car insurance. Day time TV numbed my brain. I felt like I was in a parallel universe, an outsider. The culture, thinking and behaviour that I was surrounded with were now foreign to me. I had left my conscious love bubble and I was not comfortable. I had an urge to go to India, but recognised that the timing was not right. I was in a holding pattern and tried hard to be patient.

I wanted to reconnect with my dad, so surprised him at a coffee shop in Oxford. He was attentive and loving, and we met several times after that for coffee. Sometimes we held hands, even shed a tear, secure in our love for each other. I was grateful for those fleeting moments. I told him I was leaving for India and, as always, he was silently approving, just as a father should be.

Suddenly the time was right, the signs auspicious, and I booked my flights. I had arranged to spend 40 days in an Ayurveda clinic doing Panchakarma high in the Indian hills, two hours drive from Coimbatore. Panchakarma is an ancient Indian cleansing method that does not require fasting, so I would be able to eat, which was a blessing. After that I would move on to an Ashram, I did not know which one, certain that it would be revealed to me when the time was right. I told Mummy June of my plans. She was not happy, reminding me that I would not survive a second bout of dengue in a year. I was not going to be deterred and preparations began for my next move East.

24

Holy Cow

Applying for an Indian Visa would be easy, I thought, with these regularly being issued to wealthy tourists and spiritual seekers wishing to experience a country with over a billion people and few flush toilets. I was wrong. At the local Oxfordshire post office, a pimply kid, who could not have been much more than 19, asked, "Why on earth are you going to India?"

"I am going to an ashram."

"What's an Ashram?" he asked, blankly. Misunderstanding my hesitation, his face lit up in comprehension. Winking slyly, he asked, "Is it a place you go to smoke weed and have lots of sex?"

"No," I replied politely, ignoring his crestfallen face, "It is a place where one goes to seek self, for true liberation. An Ashram is run by a resident Guru, who is normally an enlightened being."

He let this sink in, not knowing how to respond whilst he fiddled with some stamps on the counter, "I think you're mad." Came his witty retort.

I said nothing as he stared at my large golden Sri Yantra pendant. I held his gaze, expressionless, and his discomfort increased as I entering his intimate space, a strange breach of privacy that he had not experienced before. Staring, I said slowly, deliberately, "I am far madder then you will ever know." Flinching, he quickly wheeled his chair farther away from the glass.

My visa was returned 2 weeks after I sent off for it. Packing with Mummy June was easier as I had no need of the essential nail colour, hair thongs, support bras and curlers. Just some yoga gear, a couple of tops, jumpers, trainers and scarves.

Dad drove me to the airport this time.

I had co-ordinated my flight with a friend and I was going to spend a few days in Chennai first. We took off on British Airways, most of the passengers Indian, the cabin smelling strongly of curry. Best I get used to the smell. After dinner, the first class steward presented us with a huge bottle of champagne, compliments of BA. In return, we were to complete customer satisfaction forms. After one glass of our bubbly I was sloshed, happily ticking 10/10 for everything, drawing a big smiley face, adding (for good measure) I HEART BRITISH HAIRWAYS. Then fell asleep.

I woke up as we landed. I was half drunk and half hung over. It was the early hours of morning when we disembarked, the air warm, carrying a smell that I would identify as distinctly that of India. The airport epitomised third world mayhem. Everything seemed chaotic with extraordinarily long queues. Then I went to the public toilets. I thought that Thailand had prepared me for this, but India took basic facilities to a whole new level. I looked at the holes in the ground and wondered how the heck I was supposed to have a spiritual awakening without a flush toilet.

After an inordinately long wait, I spotted a mangled black Samsonite on the carousel. Outraged, I grabbed the case and examined the damage: pocket ripped; side wiring exposed; the wheel dangling. This bag was my buddy, it had travelled with me for 8 years, and this single 30-minute stint in an Indian airport had almost been the death of it.

India assaults all the senses. Outside the terminal building cars hooted, people shouted, an unrelenting riot of colour, noise, and the strong odour of exotic spices and people.

From the crowd beyond the airport fences came shouts of, "Madaamz, madaamz, you want taxi madaamz? Very small rupees," and "You want good hotel? Very nice sleepings, own shower own shower". Walking the gauntlet of mesh fencing, I felt eyes on me, on my rear, smoothly revealed in tight yoga pants. For a moment I was a celebrity, simply for being white and wearing tight pants. A man in the shoving crowd caught my eye through the mesh, connecting, "Madaam, you reesh, me poor, need rupees, no wife, no food, no cheeldren!" I stared in horror as he grinned, revealing a blood filled mouth, interspersed with orange-yellow teeth. I was rescued by our driver who told the beggar to "Fuck off" (in Hindi). With a mad laugh the old man turned away, but I insisted that he needed medical attention, his mouth wounded and bleeding. At that the driver laughed heartily, "No madaamz, that *paan.*" I thought it was a burst and bloody mouth ulcer, but found out it was Indian red chewing tobacco.

The parking lot was a jumble of cars. I spotted the first cow near a tree, munching slowly on a tuft of grass and what looked like a crisp packet. Men sat on their haunches around a make shift fire, drinking Chai, playing cards or just taking in the night sky. Our transfer car was a battered mini van. Cases in the back, we made ourselves comfortable for the journey. The dashboard was covered in beads, a worn picture of Lakshmi (Hindi Goddess of money) displayed besides the plastic head of Sathya Sai Baba, and a snow dome of New York City. Ganesh hung from the rearview mirror. Suitably protected by gods and NYC, we drove to the newly rented company apartment that my friend had been promised on her first working trip to Chennai.

We stopped near a block of apartments that looked like something out of Slumdog Millionaire, prior to the game show win. The driver helped us with our bags, trudging up the stairs, which sorely needed a new lick of paint. The rusty railings led us up to the third floor. The excited driver flung the door open and, with a sweep of his hands, said grandly, "Welcome madaamz to luxury company apart-ments, veely veely welcome."

I am not sure that my friend and I managed to stifle the horrified expressions on our faces. There was a room that may have been intended as a lounge, furnished with two uncomfortable looking, impossibly low slung and dirty paisley couches, separated by a seventies-style table. The walls were bare and stained, the kitchen reminiscent of an abattoir. It had huge steel sinks, an ancient and oversized fridge, a steel table littered with ashtrays, and was filthy. The room that I was to occupy boasted wire sprung beds and a painfully thin mattress. The curtains were paper thin, suspended from the window frame. The air conditioner took up half the wall and I stared at the dirty air filter with growing unease. I moved to the curtained window so that I could close it, hoping to block out some of the deafening street noise, but found that it was already closed. This really was a city that never sleeps. I switched the air conditioner on, filling the room with a sound of an airplane lifting off of the tarmac. I hit the off button, choosing the oppressive morning heat. The view from all windows was one befitting a slum. I thanked the Gods I was only spending three nights there.

Three days later I arrived at the small, and surprisingly clean, airport of Coimbatore. Collecting my bags I looked for a person bearing a sign with my name on it, my transfer to the Ayurvedic clinic. There was, however, no man with a sign and two hours later there was still no man with a sign. The clinic was two hours away. It was 21:00. I was to learn that India was very, very, casual. *Yesterday* meant *today*, *today* meant *tomorrow*, 09:00 was 14:00, 15:00 was 01:00, *now* could mean *never*, *yes* meant *no*, or *maybe*, but rarely did *yes* actually mean *yes*. The word, *no*, was never used with tourists.

Luckily soldiers of the British Army were at the airport to pick someone up, took pity on me, and offered me barracks, conveniently in the same village as the clinic. I found myself, once again, protected.

Early the next morning, I arrived at the clinic in a British Military vehicle. Several Indians gathered around the vehicle as I alighted, the confirmation of my name eliciting a chorus of, "Solly solly, madaamz, velly velly sollies". I wondered if someone would get the sack for not picking me up at the airport. The owner approached, a foreboding, thickly built Indian woman, the men scattering at her yell, "Stupid, stupid, solly solly, you stupid." I told her not to worry, divine intervention was at work and she looked at me suspiciously.

My luxury room was painted bright blue with cold concrete floors, a basic wooden side table, and two, very narrow, single beds. I was led proudly through the walk-in wardrobe, a narrow passage lined with shelves and a bare overhead bulb swinging slightly in the breeze. The bathroom had a flush toilet and a small bucket in the corner. Hot water in these luxury quarters was available only between 06:00 and 07:00. Not a particularly generous window, I thought.

Unpacked, I wandered around the grounds of the clinic, ready to meet my fellow retreat goers, the usual mix of suitably spiritual types. Dr Mowgli was the doctor at the clinic. I could not help humming as I bounded into the room, *Look for the bare necessities / The simple bare necessities / Forget about your worries and your strife*, a spritely tiger cub ready to begin. Dr Mowgli explained the programme which began each day at 05:00 with yoga, followed by administration of medicines, cleansing rituals and twice daily a luxurious ayurvedic body treatment. With a slew of herbal medicines in hand, I bonded with a woman, warm and welcoming, who warned of the one lecherous in-house male. I asked who he was, but she giggled, telling me not to worry as I would soon find out. I was also warned that the process of taking medicated ghee was considered difficult by all who had experienced it.

Lunch was ayurvedic food served in a myriad of little copper bowls. Pills swallowed, the afternoon treatment was a dry body scrub, followed by application of litres of sesame oil. The large traditional wooden tables were manned by two ladies at a time. Stripped down to the tiniest strip of muslin, I emerged glowing an hour later, thoroughly scrubbed. Women with their periods were not allowed to lie on the sacred table, treatments in these cases being performed on a chair, so I was to tell them when I menstruated. I winked and assured them they would be the first to know.

After yoga, it was time for dinner and at the sound of the gong I made my way into the dining room. It was a Friday night, very cold and a burst of heated air rushed out at me. Most people seemed to be already seated on the left of the hall, but on the right I spotted a man alone at a table. I headed his way, not giving the morning's warning a thought. To my delight, the elderly man seemed to be deep in prayer, but the paraphernalia around him suggested that he was not Indian. The little Jewish hat on his head explained the prayer book, a goblet with wine, a wine bottle, bread and candles. My fellow diner looked up, introducing himself as Reuben, asking if I minded if he conducted Shabbat. By this time our little table was full, all newcomers, and we agreed, adding that we would be honoured. Our food arrived and the delicious smells filled my nose. Reuben continued loudly singing his Hebrew prayers, sipping, reading and breaking bread. Fifteen minutes later I muttered, during a lull in the prayers, that I was starving and began eating a cold dinner without waiting for Reuben's approval. It took him twenty-five minutes to complete his ritual. I thought that everyone in the room was staring at me. I found out that it was unwise to sit at Rube's table on a Friday, especially if you were hungry.

When the meal ended, I asked Reuben why I had not seen him at the yoga class. "It's totally against my religion," he said, aghast. Everyone at the table was quiet. Should I point out, I wondered, that flights to Israel were cheaper than flights to India; in addition he would not have to put up with the pesky Hindu's. But I remained silent. "Would you like to come to my hut after dinner?" Reuben asked. So I had been forgiven for scoffing my food during his prayers. "Err, no, actually I am busy," I said unconvincingly. "What are you up to," he asked, grinning, his face assuming what I interpreted as a provocative look, somewhat dated. I had to think of something, fast, "Err. I am doing yoga, and some Hindi chants in the hall, you are welcome to join me." He politely declined and we went our separate ways.

Weeks into the program, with cleansing treatments, excellent food and good company, I began menstruating. Several of us had started our periods at the same time. We were forbidden from doing yoga, but thinking that no one would know, we arrived for class as usual. Our teacher, Ganesh, sat meditating, eyes furiously flickering, a semi open eyed REM, which we had become accustomed to. We settled, all seated, waiting for him to start the class. He started sniffing the air with a look of mild disgust. "Some ladies," he announced, "no good energy in room, no good, you no come to yoga for three days, you go now!" Four of us paled as he shook his head, "No good energy," he repeated with his eyes closed. Mortified, we scuttled from the room, consoling ourselves with tea and a dry biscuit. It was obvious that Hindi Hatha yoga did not favour the feminine.

 Insight: Bleeding women are not allowed on the wooden floors of the yoga hall, nor allowed to participate in yoga. Our teacher's body was so sensitive he could pick up this energy leaving us.

I was craving a full body treatment the next day, finding my massage chair ready for me. I pulled rupees and a mooncup from my bag. The ladies looked appraisingly at me, then prepared the table, ushering me into the bathroom and relieving me of 100 rupees. Apparently even a sacred table has a price.

During the fourth week it was time for the medicated ghee protocol. Dr Mowgli explained the procedure: instead of my morning medicine at 06:00, a warm cup of medicated ghee would be provided; I had to drink it quickly and try not vomit; then I had to lie down immediately and the ghee would kick in; I would feel awful and have serious diarrhoea, but would be able to crawl out of my room for soup in the evening. "How long do I do this?" I asked.

"We see, we see," said Dr Mowgli. Well, I thought, I survived *Iboga*, Dr A and the Swami so this could not be too difficult. It was not, that is until the fourth evening when I went to bed weak but with a tummy full of soup. Somewhere in the middle of the night, I woke with my body exploding in all directions. It felt as though I was inside a huge body, a hulk of a body, the Hulk itself. Wide awake and out of control I leapt from my bed and yanked open the door of my luxury room. As I stood in the unfamiliar corridor, a young blonde girl emerged from a room further down. I roared, she looked up and screamed, too late, as I pounced on her with the force of a thousand demons, ripping her body limb for limb. I devoured her, then panicked and shocked I ran back to the room, also now unfamiliar, screaming myself. I slammed the door, frenzied and berserk. I came around drenched in a pool of sweat, groaning, crying and aching. Slowly the room came into focus, but I was disorientated. Gathering up my tatty sheets, I headed out into the early morning, running to Dr Mowgli's rooms. They were locked and I shouted until someone came to find out what the commotion was. I cried, asking him to fetch the doctor, *immediately*.

"What happen Grace, what happen?" asked the good doctor a few minutes later, running to his rooms. I half sobbed, half screamed, "I killed her, I killed her."

"Who you kill?" he asked, alarmed.

"The blonde down the corridor," I moaned.

"Oh, no! Grace, no! Not lady in room 3?" his dark complexion turning pale, and he broke into a sweat.

"Not Linda, the lady from out there," I said gesticulating wildly into the atmosphere.

"No Linda?" he said, looking around.

"No Doctor, the lady was from inside but outside, in my dreams, but not dream, from another life, I am a murderer, please forgive me," I begged. It was impossible to string a coherent sentence together as I pleaded for amnesty for a crime I did, but did not commit.

"NO MORE GHEE," he barked, still sweating, "process finish, you, no more ghee," Dr Mowgli said firmly, the colour slowly seeping back into his face as he ushered me into his rooms. I sat sobbing in a chair while he scribbled furiously on my chart, handing me some herbs. "Help situation," he said. I gulped them down gratefully.

"Rest of stay, we upgrade you to luxury five star room, no pay extra!" He barked at the assistant who rushed off to get the key for my new room, with a double bed and a hot shower (most of the day.) Some of the women packed up my old room and silently moved me. Under the sedative influence of the herbs, I slept with a deepening compassion and understanding.

When I awoke the next day, violent offenders were no longer the "Other". I had been a perpetrator myself.

After six weeks my time at the clinic was up. I felt renewed, refreshed, light, clean inside and out.

Several others were heading up to an Ashram, north of Chennai. I checked online. The resident spiritual master lived in the ashram and spoke of the "Celebration of life" as a way for total liberation. He was affectionately described as a mystic full of authentic joy, love, grace with a flow of natural wisdom. I read this quote: "My teachings are nothing but my life. I cannot separate my living and my teachings. I cannot do two things at the same time. So I choose to Live! My life is nothing but a celebration. My celebration my message." As I read these words I was drawn to this incredible man, the website boasted pictures of him laughing, hugging, loving, dancing. This man lived in a realm of joy, silence, beauty, compassion and aliveness. I wanted to sit in his presence. I booked my flight for 3 days time.

There were cows everywhere, on the 2-hour drive to the Ashram from Chennai airport: cows on the highway; cows in the petrol stations; cows in the fields; cows in the parking lots. Holy Cow!

The Ashram gates opened onto an oasis of lush foliage, water features, and spacious buildings. The taxi dropped me at the beautiful reception area, and I was ushered in with my taxi driver carrying my bags. I walked in to find a picture of myself hung on the wall near the entrance. I was taken aback that I was not more "taken aback." I looked at this image, my brain finally registering that it was not an image of me, but an image of the master.

A quiet and friendly devotee checked me in and took copies of my passport. I signed the necessary forms, paid, read and agreed to the rules and asked if I could stay, until I decided to leave. "Of course," came the polite answer. I was shown to my room, on top of the reception building. It was basic and beautiful. Three spartan beds on a tiled floor with one *en suite* "bathroom" greeted me. I dropped my bags, bathed from the large bathroom bucket and went to the Ashram shop to find suitable attire for ashram life. I came away with baggy, sexless, orange linen overshirts and fisherman pants, and the obligatory white, shapeless outfit for satsang (spiritual discourse). I liked the freedom of these outfits, no hint of sexuality, just clothes for the "soul" purpose of comfort, covering the body and shielding it from the sun.

Lunch time was a delight of seekers buzzing, singing, or in silent reflection around numerous tables. The normal buffet table heaving with fresh vegetables, *dhal,* rice, fruit and spring water. We ate slowly, conversations kept to a minimum, connecting with our eyes, nodding, acknowledging and silently greeting. A current shot through the air when Guruji joined us for lunch. I watched him as he warmly and openly greeted, hugged and embraced everyone. I wondered whether he would notice me and what he would do. I was a little nervous as he laid eyes on me and immediately moved to welcome me. In his presence I felt an overwhelming warmth, a deep compassion, a knowing that he would love and accept me. His huge energy field left me humbled as he touched my face and moved on. This man was different, he was not ordinary, he was a spectacular example of the "Christ consciousness." Even in his wake I felt changed, knowing we can all exist in this state, knowing that if we did our world would be utterly different.

I sat in silence, guitars were being strummed, ladies bustling in the kitchen, the lines to wash our own plates and cutlery forming. I was in the right place at the right time with the right people, feeling the perfection I walked back to my room bare foot.

Insight: Guruji is a generic, respectful and affectionate name for a spiritual master.

On the first day at the ashram, I joined my fellow seekers, all dressed in baggy white clothing, in the Satsang hall at 4:00pm. We sang devotional songs, loud, strong, clear, all devoted to the Gods inside us, the Gods in nature, the earth, our teacher, each other. Thirty minutes later Guruji was there to answer questions, as opposed to pontificating on a topic of his choice.

A German asked why people came to an Ashram, and how did it help to liberate them. I thought it a silly question, one that he should have cleared up before the flight from Germany to India. But then I realised that I had no answer to this question myself. I was there because I felt compelled – no real reason – I wanted a different experience.

Guruji answered in his rich, thick Indian accent, broken English and lots of repetition, "An Ashram is a place where people go for inner transformation. Normally an Ashram is based around a Guru who is realised and people gather around that Guru to learn to realise or to experience a realised person. When a person comes to the Ashram, for example he is coming from his normal life. Whatever you call 'normal'. Say you are coming from Norway, and if you are totally happy and content you will be and stay in Norway because this is what you want and you are right to stay there.

"If you are looking for 'Self' you want to find yourself or you want to experience something else. That means you are looking for a different experience to the one you are having. We do not have to compare your previous experience as good or bad, but we have to accept you are trying for another experience. So you are living in Norway and now you are in India. Now you are coming to an Ashram for example. You are trying to experience something else and there is no comparison. You cannot compare why India is not like Norway. Why are there lots of cows in the middle of the road? In Norway there are no cows in the middle of the road. *Unconsciously you connect the present with the past.* Now you are trying to make India like Norway, from where you are trying to get away."

He explained that India is different from Norway, and that is why we have come here, to experience something different, so we must stop comparing. He said we must open our eyes to a new way of being and a new experience.

But as he spoke, the penny started to drop. Well not so much drop, as spin in a circle, ready to drop. If I did not like my old life, I had to accept that I had come to the ashram for something new. Here things were radically different. My reality was that I was living in harmony, in paradise, in a love bubble, with free beings in a safe space, but my patterning and conditioning was still in the past. Every moment I would make comparisons to my old life. His advice was to drop the past for a while. It is Ashram culture that we speak only our names and if we speak, we speak only of the present. Silence badges can be freely attached to our robes so that others respect our right for silence. I thought the silence was about peace and tranquillity. But it is also so that we do not engage in conversations of the past, where we are strongly identified with the labels we have given ourselves: lawyer, mother, wife, girlfriend, vegan, cancer patient, blonde, car owner, house owner, bright person, slim person; and a hundred and one others.

It was liberating to be free of labels.

So the first lesson was to stop speaking about the past, then I would eventually stop thinking about the past, until I no longer identified myself with careers, names and strong beliefs. All this melted into simply being in the now, fully present in every moment. There was no pressure to do, impress or compare.

I felt space and bliss. Living in the now was living in the flow. Doing whatever that moment required me to do. Not thinking or dreaming of what tomorrow may ask of me. This becoming my new path.

Guru Sri Vast wanted us to be consciously free. Freedom can only exist when the mind is still, when we have no thoughts about the past or the future. Everything leading up to that moment had prepared me well for this, the more I was in the now, the more blissful my life started becoming. I also knew that a calmness of the body creates a calmness of the mind. No more rushing, dashing, moving and hurrying. There was nowhere to go, only to be.

After satsang it was dinner under the warm Indian skies, the climate was mildly humid as the ashram was near a coastal town. Tranquillity settled in our micro community, as we moved in unorchestrated harmony. To bed early and alarm set for a 4:30 wake up.

My alarm gently woke me. I arose and gazed out of my top floor window to be greeted by India before the dawn. The sky was light blue and encrusted with a million brilliant stars, the birds song infiltrating my sleepiness. I dressed, walked downstairs for the early morning tea ceremony. Other seekers, in white, moved consciously, slowly, towards the same destination. My bare feet padded softly on the dusty and cool ground. I raised my eyes, noticing the organic gardens bursting with growing food. I past the orchards next, enveloped in a bed of long grass, with young citrus fruit growing on every tree. I saw hammocks strung up in the orchards, learning that Guruji had erected them for contemplation within nature. The road ahead was peppered with white linen trousers and soft deliberate shuffles, heading towards the transformed satsang hall. From a hundred metres away I could see the watery moat and the wooden bridge leading to the hall. Hundreds of candles lined the bridge and a huge paper star hung above the doorway, through which I could see the warm glow of candles. Over the wooden bridge and into the hall, the sense of unspoken community fuelling me, I sat cross legged in one of many rows facing an unknown partner. We prayed to the day, to the unfolding, to the Universe, to love and to each other. After prayers, one cup of warm ginger tea was placed in front of us and in unison we drank to the beginning of another magical moment.

That is how I should start every day, I thought.

Keen to share my stories about the "super powers" that I had unwittingly acquired at Tantra School, I sought out the Guru. Over lunch I proudly described my powers, hoping to elevate my "spiritual being" status. His laugh was deep and loud, saying, "Grace, that stuff, only more label, keep you from God. No need to be distracted by powers." He gave me a loving look, as at a child with all the potential the Universe has to offer. I scuttled away, underpants firmly staying on the inside of my sexless ashram robe and my Ego once again put firmly back in its place.

The days and weeks melted into one another. Food fresh from the gardens, water from a local spring, friends being made, music composed and a peace manifesting from beyond. The teachings from Guruji filled with throaty laughter, ah ha moments, tears and hugs. Profound truth left him and filled us, he urged us to go, to live, to expand, to love. His message was simple, only our minds and Ego's fighting this unfamiliar concept.

When the time was right I felt it necessary to leave this place of love, to cultivate a new life, different from the days of "the London drain."

My only wish was to expand into life with my heart open.

I had witnessed many people leaving the Ashram. There is a tradition that the musicians and seekers gather around the departing taxi and sing. They sing for the person leaving, wishing them love, joy and prosperity. It is always a warm occasion, but not without tears. I was a relative "newbee" to this Ashram and being a little shy, only told the reception staff and few of the friends of my departure. My taxi arrived, I slipped out of that evening teachings, packed the taxi and headed down the long drive way. Just before the gates I saw a lady running down the road behind me shouting my name. I told the taxi driver to "put foot," but he merely hit the brakes. She rushed to the car, out of breath and asked "are you leaving?",

"Yes"

"Guruji wants to see you before you go, do you have time?"

I walked back into the teaching space, a hundred eyes on me. Guruji opened his huge arms and enfolded me, holding me and my untold fears of the future, simply giving them silently to God. His warmth was all encompassing and he held my face and wished me well. Looking deep into his eyes I knew he was right. With tearful eyes I thanked everyone for being with me and slowly and deliberately made eye contact with each person in this large circle, my hands in prayer position, lingering longer on those I knew well. I turned back to Guruji who gave me a signed copy of his teachings. He gazed warmly at me, as if upon his own child, as I left the space.

Walking into the night I heard someone say, "I can't believe Grace has left." Guruji laughed a deep laugh and said, "Grace has not left, a person called Grace is leaving, but Grace will always be here."

In the back seat of this noisy Indian taxi, I silently stared out at the night sky. Crocodile tears rolled down my cheeks, the enormity of my journey beginning to register. I had fundamentally altered the entire course of my life. My experiences of God, death and sex setting me on a trajectory previously unimagined.

My old city life felt like a dream playing in a theatre I no longer frequent. The taxi bumped down the corrugated dirt road, whilst the "Ganesh-on-a-string" swung wildly from the rear view mirror. The tears did not stop and I felt the age old question rise again, "who am I now?"

I let this question sink in as my driver turned onto a quiet highway. I wound down the window a little and let the warm Indian night engulf me. I lay my head back on the black vinyl head rest and took in my surroundings. As I spotted a few cows ambling in the slow lane, a quiet peace filled me. My tears stopped flowing, and a tangible warmth spread through me. In my inner stillness, the answer found me " you are the same person you have always been but never dared to see."

ACKNOWLEDGEMENTS

I wanted to write a very professional acknowledgements page. So I googled what I should say and who I should include. Apparently I have to thank everyone involved in the production of the book, which would be my editor and book cover designer and the Acknowledgments page would be a sentence. In order to bulk this sentence up I could also extend my thanks to my Team: my MAC Book Air; my kitchen table; my one comfy chair; my over worked kettle; and my trusty dressing gown that kept the frost bite at bay. I could include thanks to my local coffee shop for its WiFi, hot food and doubling as an office/meeting place.

So in the interests of not being brief, I want to say some public thank you's. If you are not one for Oscar speeches and the like, I strongly suggest you turn the pages until you reach Chapter One because I feel like gushing.

My life is an intricate web of inter connectedness. I am who I am largely because of this web, and the skilful guidance of an unseen force. Thousands of people, circumstances, events and situations have shaped me and this book. It seems an impossible task to do justice to all of its contributors. I will endeavour, however, to briefly mention some of them.

My journey to the East allowed me to connect with people who are living an extraordinary life, bravely exploring the scariest territory of all: The Inner Terrain. Alessia Follador, my sister, thank you for walking with me. To Anne Marie Woodall for telling your story which allows me to tell mine. To Becky Nodding, Carl Maxfield, Chrstina Klioumis, Irina Egorova, Josh Dharma, Jacqui Ashley, Nick

Dilks, Gila, San Bao, Rocio Gaborit and Sasha Tovstik for cohabiting on a very small island with me and being part of the fabric of life. To Stuart Snell for the White Book and all things "Ayu". To James G Delglyn: How could I be Grace without you? To Barrie Musgrave for being a wizard, for assisting me when no one else could. To Wayne "release me" for your powerful work. To Mish Shakti, you took me in and shared your story, which left me speechless. You are an incredible human being. To Juliet and Jiva Carter and The Template. Thank you for disseminating the truth and following the inner voice. To Saeed Khan, for breathing into me and with me. For John Nilsen for being awesome, for being a stable masculine presence and in service. You are my Captain Fantastic. To Jean Pierre Le Blanc for coaching the Goddess out of me, for your wisdom, kindness, jacuzzi's and never giving up. To Tao Nelson for rocking my world, for giving me Shiva, for holding me, for being my safe space, for seeing my seer. You have my heart.

To Dr A and Dr William, for helping me to overcome my fears, for helping to cleanse my body, for reflecting my inner neurotic, inner paranoid, for seeing the monkeys in my head and calling me on my crap. What a gift, what a painful process. To a woman who listened in the early days with compassion and energy, helping me to awaken, Kerry-Lyn Stanton Downes. To Laura Collett for being a friend, for wiping my bloody noses and always smiling. To Tarryn von Oppell for your friendship and nutritional support, Pret coffee dates and listening.

To Annabel Nicholls, I love you, when I think of you I smile, thank you for your sultry voice, your healing hands and your friendship and for sharing Bean Bag Bohemia with me in your James Bond number.

To Aurelia Gezynska, you captured my heart, you loved me and made me raw chocolate tarts, you are a Goddess, my sister and an angel. To Elicia Marie Woodford, for being the Warrior Goddess, for your commitment to detoxification, cleansing and shedding, you inspire me. To Jayne Hedger for your laughter, your joy, your madness and your freedom. Thank you for meditating with me, for being a sounding board and for living a life less ordinary. To Gabriel Rymberg, for being my angel, for being gentle, tender and moving me. Brother (formerly Patrick O'Connor), thank you for your masculine strength, your work and your commitment to growth, oneness and love. To Todd McPherson, for helping to open me, for being honest with me and loving me exactly as you did. To Stuart Ringer for walking a path, for following your dreams.

To Jo Rowkins, my sister, for your utter love, your generosity with your life, your home and the Golden Chariot. You taught me about the feminine, about womanhood and how to make the best green smoothies. Julie Rousseau and Jody West, for swimming in the warm dolphin filled Bahamian oceans with me under a sky filled with stars.

To my mum, who nurtured, cared for me and loved me. Who has offered a gift of truly unconditional love, thank you for being my mum. I know our souls will mingle through time. To my father for being solid, being stable, for always encouraging me to be the sovereign individual. Thank you for always swimming against the stream. To Don for being my earth brother, for living my life with me, for being generous, for being calm in times of instability. For the company you created; it is an extension of your passion for preventive medicine and wellness. To my earth family, I love you always.

To my Cape Town sisters for sitting in circle with me, for sweating with me and just being. To Cindi Meltz and Warren Bezuidenhout for having faith in me and for hosting my first reading. To The Dawn Penny, my light and my fairy, for being utterly divine, for rebirthing me and holding a space which has grown me. Thank you. To Sonica Kirsten, my rock and my sister. For teaching me, keeping me "sane", for helping me to decode my dream world. Thank you for stilling my inner waters and walking on the beach with me. To Anabu for being a wonderful, joyful dog who chases waves and is always pleased to see me. To Gary Simons, for being in service to all women, for being a wise man, a superb coach and an attentive listener.

To everyone I have mentioned and the thousand in and around me, you have been with me in my darkest hour, given without expectation. You humble me, you teach me. You make me want to be greater than I am. You give me faith in humankind and you graciously remind me that my life counts, that I am loved, that I matter.

I have an odd feeling I may have left someone important off my list in some horrible error. If you are that person, you know I love you and I blame the mad inner author.

To two people who feature prominently in the book
Mark England, for being my brother, for protecting me, pushing me and giving me the opportunity to look at my story, my past and my dark side. For doing the craziest stuff I can imagine, for feeding my inner adventurer. Thank you for helping to shatter the stories that bound me. You are my family, I love you, thank you.

Anna Suvarova, my angel, my heart, my cosmic soul sister, you have lifted me towards the light. You have been real with me, even when it hurt. You loved me without condition. You felt like home, you nurtured me during my darkness days on earth. You never gave up on me. I will adore you until the end of time.

To the people who have helped shape this book directly
To Susan Walker, an old friend, who has listened whilst I rant, who has been a quiet and calming force in my life. Thank you for your friendship and for planting the seed of this book, for that is where this began.

To Debra Ann Doyle my sister, my friend, my protector, my Batman. You are a fierce and fair force in the Universe. Your generous spirit has taught me many things. You have helped when nobody else could or would. Your thoughtfulness and willingness to assist has saved me. I am deeply, deeply grateful for your energy and love in my life. I love you and your enormous heart. Thank you for being my number one fan.

To Catherine Williams, without your wisdom, patience and gentleness, this book would not have been written. You sat for hours and hours reading, uncovering and helping me to dig deeper into my life and experience. You gave me faith in my story. Thank you for working on your stuff and reminding me that when I "do my hardest thing" I give permission to everyone else to do theirs.

To Catherine Christie, your passion and belief in my work has encouraged and fuelled it. Thank you for delivering the angelic message that helped to create this book. Your generousity and support during this process has meant a lot to me. To Cameron Christie for listening to me read and for loving my words.

To my editor Patricia Crain (a.k.a. Shekina). You have made this into what it is. Your work and wisdom in that area of tantra, life, healing and all things esoteric have been invaluable. I felt you truly understood my story. Your work has astounded me.

To Sarah Scott, who initially gave a face to my words.

To Toby Newsome, for creatively completing this process.

To Africa; You humble me

To Cape Town: I could not have written this book anywhere but at home.

11502306R00143

Printed in Great Britain
by Amazon.co.uk, Ltd.,
Marston Gate.